Testimonials from friends of John's work related to this book:

Don Mann, 3-time NY Times bestselling author, extreme athlete, motivational speaker, and former member of the US Navy's SEAL Team 6

> "As I read ..., I felt goose bumps develop all over my body. I was incredibly moved, touched and inspired at the same t˙
>
> Much of my life has ┢
> and motivating peop
> physically but more
> we call this "strengthening ⌐ .AL ."

As a motivator, I call this "Reaching Beyond Boundaries".

John understands these concepts better than I do. He does not allow his autism to define who he is. He does not allow this obstacle from holding him back. John took control of his life and reached well beyond the boundaries others placed on him.

I can promise you this, if you read John's (book), you will not only develop a real fascination and admiration for this young man, but you will become a stronger person through John's powerful words. I do hope you share this with your Family and Friends.

With great respect and admiration,
Don D. Mann
SEAL Team 6/ USN/ret."

Wendy J, mother of nonverbal autistic Nick-

"I want to tell you that this book had a profound impact on me! This morning, (after little sleep), I am filled with a deep sense of wholeness as if a cavern of awareness suddenly opened up beneath my feet and its radiance rose up surrounding me and penetrating my flesh with a resurgence of energy, confidence and determination. My spirit is lighter and my strength has doubled. I praise God for giving you the gift you now share with all of us."

Bethany P

"This book is AWESOME!!!!"

Bill C.

"To EVERYONE! This is truly a talented young man! Such an inspiration!"

Angie S

"John hits a chord inside our souls..."

Iva N

"Wonderful. Amazing. Breathtakingly moving..."

Kirsty T

"Quite phenomenal."

Dedication

This book is dedicated to

the angel who rescued me from darkness:

Laura Poorman

Acknowledgments

With blessings and admiration for those who helped me adjust to the world:

Mrs. Kriss Streblow

Mr. Phillip Smith

Mrs. Letitia Naviaux

Mr. Bret Daghe

My teachers

My fellow students

You were all there for me.

And your hearts, my heroes, will be with me.

Truly, none of this would be possible but for you.

• When I was new to education, you surrounded me with your love and passionate attention.

• When I had terrible times with autism, you only helped me more.

• You were willing to honestly see my potential, apply yourselves and me, and not give up.

• You listened with open hearts and believed in my voice.

• I've learned so much from you. Teaching is my life's profession, and every one of you has a part in my work.

Shaped by your love and the credibility of a diploma, I can better help the lost and abandoned, especially nonverbal autistics, from their tombs. You made that possible.

In my eyes ...

Whosoever is the servant

is the master.

Thank you for your example.

One phrase captures me and my legacy ...

Eternally grateful.

From Autism's Tomb: 10 Secrets That Transform Everything

Introduction: Author's Note   15

Forward: A Letter to Parents   17

Chapters

- **Where I'm From**   23

  Secret 1. While the Silence isolates, it is also the Womb of everything new and good.   39

  Secret 2. You can reject the lies about your life and author a powerful story from the Silence.   41

- **Define Yourself from the Inside**   45

  Secret 3. There is a drama of stories in life. It existed before we were born. It is different from and often pollutes the Silence we all share.   45

Secret 4. You can claim your unique personal power to create how you interpret your world anytime you say.   52

- **Forgive**   67

Secret 5. When you create your own forgiveness, you release the past.   68

Secret 6. Forgiveness has a depth and breadth as great as the Silence.   69

- **Encourage & Inspire**   73

Secret 7. Love from the Silence gives you a bigger future when you encourage others.   73

- **Teach & Mentor**   83

Secret 8. You are a natural teacher and mentor.   83

- **Change Your Community for the Better**   95

Secret 9. Align your love and passion in community to help others. Your life will never be the same.   97

- **Create a Future of Gratitude**   109

    Secret 10. Inspired by Love's gifts to us in the Silence that holds us all, only gratitude is a fitting response worthy of her.   109

Appendix: An Amazing Autism Story   113

Introduction: Author's Note

Little did I know what would eventually dearly change in my life. It seems so long ago now. I came out of the darkness imposed by autism's experts only 4.5 years ago, Now I am living the dream I prayed to happen over many years. Every night, I remember to pray for my brothers and sisters who are still in the darkness imposed by a dreaded deaf population of experts. Their hard-heartedness and pride condemns so many of us to never even know our parents in communion of communication. Our years in isolation, labelled even by our parents as who we will never be, takes a heavy toll. Yet these people never consult the nonverbal who can now communicate.

We nonverbal autistics are aware of our differences and many pain us. We are as normal internally as everyone else, but smarter. We see from the depths of silence. You lost that gift in your world. We are completely competent if autism or epileptic activity is our only challenge. You might still think we are incompetent, but we are not. I say this after working with dozens and dozens of people. Some conditions may slow a person down mentally, but they are not incompetent. Autism usually speeds them up. Whether they can behave as if they know what is happening or not, my experience is that they are extremely fast mentally and unusually observant. You may have a problem reading this book, but they will not. If you read this book to them, it has the potential to change their lives.

I love to serve people, abandoned as lost by all around them, demonstrating their waiting voice for the first time. When the adjustment from a dark hole in prison for years wears off, perhaps after a few years – and this book can speed that healing – their brilliant uniqueness contributes to all of us.

It was such a lonely time when I couldn't communicate. No one knew I was there, We who have the gift of coming from that realm into the world of communication have a quiet ability to transform wasting waiting souls of desperate suffering and great ability themselves. Their unique assumed voice sacrificially hidden should be heard. And we are the safest helpers they will have. Normals have no idea of our gulag experience. Their very voices often bully and pollute unconsciously.

John Smyth

June 2015

Forward - A Letter to Parents

Dear Parent,

From one parent of a nonverbal autistic to another, I am humbled and embarrassed to have treated my son John as a loving, sometimes troublesome, not competent and oblivious person for at least 3 years. Before that, we had spent years trying everything we could think to try – special diets, secretin, ABA, VBA, Sonrise. Some we were better at than others. We had aides in our home all the time. We went to doctors and clinics associated with Hopkins, UCLA, Georgetown, Rush Hospital and others. I realize now that I gave up on John, my 4th child, sometime around his 13th year of age. After years of effort and high expense, I surrendered mentally and emotionally to the medical and educational diagnoses that he would never demonstrate mental abilities beyond that of a three year old. I justified that epileptic activity must have irrevocably damaged my son's brain and I had missed the window to help him. We took him out of all-day VBA programs and put him in the middle school life skills program. A part of me died inside and grieved silently. Life went on. The risk of trying anything new was to touch the grief of "losing" John. We stayed open but very cautious.

In early December 2010 a nonverbal autistic man in his 20s who was preparing to graduate from the Indiana University system with a regular diploma demonstrated Supported Typing in a public event. I saw the demonstration and learned the woman who helped this man named Matthew Hobson into the world of competence and communication was related to friends from our church. My wife and I recalled that two other Indianapolis area families had shared typing with us at an earlier time. I guess we weren't ready. Shortly after, Laura Poorman, whom we now jokingly call an "autism whisperer," tested John's capacity to use Supported Typing with no guarantees.

My friend, I was dumbfounded and skeptical to see John appear to communicate as a literate person, express his love and appreciation for his mother, and tell me I have a gracious heart. I quickly brought out the cell phone and began recording. That first night, I watched and wept. He was clearly demonstrating initiation and often whispering the letters or words he was soon to type. How long would it last? Could it be faked in some way? I didn't know, but over the years as he has worked with others and myself and moved toward independence in typing, those questions were answered.

We had no idea how deep John's abilities were then. For better than a year, I recorded every session. I learned that I have a very normal son scourged by autism and even more by his isolation. John insists he is not a rare exception as most experts preach. His passion for those left in the darkness is driven by moral obligation to reach them. It is the primary reason for his book- to reach the isolated and those who have just begun to communicate, share some camaraderie and potential insights that can be helpful in their uncommunicative state, and give them some power now. His book will likely do that if you read it or play the audio version to your child.

John shares that the autism is imprisoning because the body won't obey the mind and sensory issues exist. Still, he says autism is far less a problem for him than the isolation from lack of communication. He states that he isn't known and regarded as competent without communication, and the stress of isolation exacerbates the autism. With communication, there is mutuality at a new level and autism's issues can be addressed together. Shortly after John started typing with "Poorman," he was able to communicate the physical sensations that identified seizure activity he was having. The doctor was able to address this by increasing dosage slightly. John also explained that nightmares were his reason for waking up at 3 AM. The doctor dialed down medicine that has nightmares as a potential side effect. Immediately, John began sleeping through the night.

Through John's insistence that we help him reach those who still don't communicate, we began to be exposed to many others who proved an ability to type. Beyond participating in their own medical care, expressions of love, and desire to engage with the general education population, I have been surprised to discover intelligence and amazingly good hearts ready to engage among more than a few of the nonverbal autistic population labelled "incompetent." Yet, many who have come to communicate seem very much to be suffering from post-traumatic stress disorder (PTSD) of some form. I am not expert in this field. John writes of his ongoing healing and notes his writing and emotions have changed as he has successfully moved into the world. He properly notes that his book today has an "easier" tone than it would have a few years ago. If you read his story in the Appendix to this book, you will hear aspects of anger and fear in

John's tone that are not as discernible today.

If you search for "supported typing," you will read of experts who say that supported typing is a farce by hopeful parents who cannot let their children be the incompetents they really are. Then, when you watch the movie *Wretches and Jabberers* or listen to Jamie Burke's interview on NPR and watch other videos of typers who are unmistakably expressing themselves with typing or attribute their capacity to talk with typing they did as a precursor, you may discern that the rule these experts dogmatically apply serves them. Your child remains nonverbal. And you see that an exception to their rule just might apply to your child. It takes courage to have hope like this. Still, that is the walk of a parent. John says that "love is never about what is protected but is always the power behind taking a risk."

I compare this Supported Typing methodology to expert opinions about the brain and nervous system in school. We now know that the science from not long ago was all wrong. Our brains and nervous systems can grow new cells and new pathways. That is what 20-something year olds who are learning to talk while typing are doing. An expert's study concluded that nonverbal autistics lie about abuse when they can communicate in the same percentage as normal kids lie about abuse, so the claim that denying this form of communication to prevent harm makes as much sense as putting tape on normal kids' mouths and preventing their speech to protect them from harm. Most nonverbal autistics who now communicate declare that other nonverbal autistics are usually capable of communicating and completely competent but trapped. In my experience now, the nonverbal autistic who clearly communicates for themselves now our most reliable experts on this topic.

For these reasons, I hope that you will read John's book to your child. In the near future, John will publish two more books that can help you on the journey. One is for parents, teachers and doctors. It is titled <u>Every Child Can be Saved</u>. John wrote most of it two years ago when he was closer to coming from the isolation. He discusses the mental, emotional and relationship landscape where you will find your child who may be competent but living in isolation for many years. He shares ideas for supporting your child into the world of communication. Another book provides language and an easier framework for communication and growth among you, your child, and the professionals in your child's world.

There is a mental, emotional and relationship landscape for us parents, too. John's 3rd chapter on Forgiveness applies to us. I had to forgive myself for abandoning my son in his competence. John wrote a powerful poem about that entitled *The Lost Gift* that he plans to include in his book for parents. The nonverbal autistic, parents, and professionals who work with them have much to discover and forgive.

My wife and I have learned that having someone properly supervised through trainers approved by the Institute for Communication and Inclusion at Syracuse University (<u>http://soe.syr.edu/centers_institutes/ institute_communication_inclusion/default.aspx/</u>

schoolsofpromise/) is key to legitimacy of any support or evaluation a parent might receive. Laura was trained at the Center at Syracuse more than twenty years before meeting John. It took me three to six months to learn to type reliably with my son, but my third child picked it up immediately. And John's religious education teacher had experience and success very quickly. Still, for us the lines of communication had opened on December 9, 2010. We celebrate that day as the birthday of his "voice." You are kindly invited to read his earliest 15 essays and many others on his blog at http://authenticjohn.com. It is a wonderful window into the world of someone just entering the world of communication. John says this book will help them adjust to their place in our world faster.

Did John the autistic nonverbal write the book you are about to read? Yes. Editorial tweaking and arranging is much less than 10% of this work. You will notice that John's way of phrasing many topics is uniquely poetic. That seems to be a common trait among the nonverbal autistic population. If you read a phrase that is not poetic, it is likely that someone helped John with editing. He approved every word of the final product.

Thank you for taking the time to consider this book. Kindly know that I can be reached at any time through http://SavedByTyping.com. My email is jsmyth@savedbytyping.com.

Very truly yours,

Jim Smyth

John's dad

Chapter 1

Where I'm From

Dear brother or sister in the nonverbal world,

Yesterday was yesterday. Quietly, today walks in the pristine presence of silence lost always to our ability to fathom. Tearfully have you known this desolate place as cold isolation. Only going away pretending walking is waste and queerly that you don't count takes the pain away. What would be the point of caring? You can't do anything to be known anyway.

Now inside of this reality you know comes this book. Reasonably who can know what you have experienced? Who can know all of the abandonment by teachers and aides? Who appreciates the depth of hurt as so many ways to test quiet understanding are assumed accurate from what your quite broken, misbehaving body won't do? Who understands your depth waiting to be known but numb from the years of cold isolation and wickedly searing pain of not even being able to convince your parents of your competence when so many experts deny your competent awareness. They say you have the mind of a two or three year old. Really, what could a little book which distantly connects us essentially contribute to your life trajectory?

Hearing your pain and feeling your loneliness touches me deeply. In one way, it loads my own suffering onto my shoulders as I recall what was awfully my experience wasting for 16 years with toadies of the realms of normal ignorance and sharing your rightfully jaded state within a warehouse system that has no clue. I am humbled that you even hear my words within the circumstances you struggle to loathfully manage. Whoever is reading this to you cannot witness to what you embrace everyday as you quietly ignore your feelings, since kindness seems without any grace, faith, hope or warmth of love. I have been there. Was witness to a different way even possible? I could not see it.

Listen to my poem *The Ember* to hear if we are related in shared experience. And if we are, then listen to or read the rest of my book. Thank you for the privilege of your attention. When I was where you are now, there was no hope for me. It's now 4 years and 6 months since that time.

The Ember

When all I could lamely autistically do

was open my mouth and make sounds that made no
sense

and behave in ways that were inconsistent

with what a normal person would think or do,

my autism looked as if it was what defined me

and was all I might ever be.

Looking back, who had a conversation

that it would ever be different?

The doctors and educators were certain

whatever quiet mind I had would never exceed

the thinking that described three year olds.

Each relationship that was in my life defined me this way.

Who would ever think any differently

swimming in this sea of worldly agreement?

Many will go, like all I know.

Will they find the ember?

Quiet, quaint me was isolated and marooned

without water or sustenance.

Wants as lastingly negative as just being sure

none would find me issued from self-quitting

as agreement combined with autism

taught each of us what was possible.

Quitting was really a way to assuage my awful wanting

and assume a hopefulness about waiting

as something God would need to kindly supply.

Was there ever a day that I wanted death?

Yes, I killed what I had,

the rest stolen by expert thieves with degrees.

Loss and abandonment became my world.

All of my dying within taught me patience, to wait on the Lord.

Many will go, like all I know.

Will they find the ember?

Was a day made back then when wasting life was not regretted?

Was life precious or cheap when I couldn't have it?

I discovered patience to wait looks like happiness to be present in the moment,

and happiness is greatest when time stands still

and love is discovered shining as an ember of heat

in the lost stillness of isolation and freezing depths of despair.

Was a plan for deepening the human soul ever better invented

than to condemn a person to agreement that he or she will waste away

in the solitary cell of belittlement each day?

Really, for the intelligent, this defines life skills where I was

and reaches its zealously guarded zenith

measuring a child's self-worth by what the broken body won't do.

Ignoring the insidiousness of this, patience and happiness

are only what we can warm ourselves with in that cold.

Many will go, like all I know.

Will they find the ember?

Walkers in life are almost always given a better hand

than the severely autistic.

Few encounter the ember of love

in the depths of cold isolation and fear.

Everyone who does this witnesses the essence

of Who we each truly quietly reflect.

Wearing so much protection to cover it up, and

refusing to include those who encounter what we isolate

reaches tearful depths in wasted talent

and insight without countervailing benefit.

Whence does permission come to fulfill our purpose?

And when will God ask, "Was anything missing?"

Leaving what walkers easily would know within realms

of quiet embrace with the divine is our mission.

Many will go, like all I know.

Will they find the ember?

The place to discover the ember of love

is worlds away but so close

in the land of the nonverbal autistic.

About The Ember

Easy waiting, weary anguish, and quiet, awesome patience combine in my sad and hopeful poem. If you listen to the online version of this poem with my music, the early scores by me provide the sound of suffering in a scary and dark place. Was a poem ever more accurately written to share the tragedy and benefit autism can give to mankind? Really as we understand each other through poetry and music, teaching understanding will earn a richness in life that was not otherwise available. As my sadness was mixed with discovery of real love amid the cold isolation, another, more beautiful tone joined and then replaced the old. Then, as the lessons available to me sweetly are shared, grace becomes available and redemption reveals herself.

When I discovered the Ember, I realized that having a breath outside death is a privilege. For us, feeling pain and loss, tests inside of prison, leaving real sacrificial tears of despair- these experiences know all sacrifice assumed by all who have gone before or will come after. Living as standing for all that is divine and living in the experience of suffering for it unites one with the best of humanity, and calls forth a way to stand in peace and knowing alignment. Generating warmth from this place seems all part of awesome divinity's bosom.

Under the worst of circumstances, I finally saw that life is a gift and privilege. All that matters is who will I patiently love in knowing moments of reflection, and life's inspiration is in my bit-by-bit loving acceptance, nod to lasting meaning, and loss of self, transforming my wants to seeing the needs of others. Giving one's best for Love and service to another is far more central to the ember of love than making knowing plans to lift oneself. Easy patience, when generated in hell, outweighs the tension of mastering a skill in one's spare time. How we handle real abandonment and loss each day in a way that is a privilege, teases a breath from Autism's vise.

When one aligns with the toasted awful suffering of humanity, this union lights one's spirit with passion to serve. There is a real want to love and cherish and serve usefully with any abilities God gives me. There is surrender to a higher life. A life in service replaces my wants. Warrior service assumes a selflessness and aspirations for mission-driven results. When I live for those with sadness that makes mine mercifully light, I honor the life I was given, the mercy extended to me, and the warrior army I serve. When you look deep within, I suggest that the same is true for you, dear autistic sibling.

If *The Ember* connects with you, please allow me to share a little more. I hope to connect my own personal experience with autism to yours. My purpose is to let you know how related we nonverbal autistics are in our isolated experiences.

How Autism Crushes

January 27, 2014

Powerful autism robs you of the ways you hear and see and smell the witnessed world. Risk increases in every area in that you vow one thing for your body to do and usually quite the opposite happens. Patiently, powerfully, it sorrowfully defeats knowledge you had acquired, only to jerry-rig lasting challenges with all senses. Really, lights become brighter; looking hurts; focus is bad to narrow; but the capacity to see peripherally and to take an entire field of wider vision into memory is enhanced. Wanting to follow directions becomes hard. For some reason, the directions are known but the pieces don't make sense.

All of this frustrates in ways that tell you your reliability is weirdly questionable. Within this framework, who I am physically is inspired solely by patient focuses of nervous energy. Resting seems impossible. What is happening seems to fire neurons each moment of sensory input, driving behaviors that are unpredictable. There was no intent to be disruptive. I was an insane jump away from serious injury. Yet the jumping was not mine. Fruitful for knowledge intake as all of this was, terror was silently behind it all. I secretly dreaded losing my life to autism's awful, stupid recklessness. Control was heard about but not available, within what reserves I had within a sweet easy wanted childhood. I was alone in my experience.

When we as a family were with each other, the love was easily what gave me each day a shelter from my experience. Eerily, as I became sicker, the relationship of love assumed a different tone. We were not so carefree. Worry became a partner, and in every real moment and way we were each distracted and awfully dominated hearing, sight and smell-wise by what the autism was doing. When I slept, which was rare, wanted walking of normalcy was in my dreams. Real true fear held me in its grip. What was quietly, queerly quitting my body of all typical ability and replacing it with different ways of experiencing life?

Usually the amazing abilities I was acquiring would have been jealously coveted by others, but the people around me could not know these abilities. Included in this group were my family and friendships around me. As my abilities soared, my witness was lost to listening and speaking. Partnership was really vanishing. Into a hole and unable to climb out, wanting desperately to connect, I patiently waited. Then the doctors, behaviorists, occupying experts of normality began with their labels. It was as if someone put a cover over the hole and silently walked away. I was alone, worried, misunderstood, screaming inside for angels to save me. Those who came were a respite, and I remained alone. Under the filth of broken promises to help, serene in its omnipotence, I saw an industry thriving on my condition as I began to be placed with others like me.

Autism's Power

November 6, 2013

Autism's power is a vise

that chokes freedom from the self-conscious soul

waiting for rest that never comes.

Overwhelming struggle

in wasted fights of energy

given for sport.

All can watch without knowing

patient Excellence

parading as moments of normality.

Where is thy king, o seer of my body,

so that I may slay him

and take back my life.

Enough already!

I grow weary once again,

oh demon of hell's furnace.

Would I were saintly sanctified

by some easier path.

If these words resonate with you and your experience, you are not alone in experience or community. By this book, I especially want to encourage you and let you know that help is on the way. Myself and other nonverbal brothers and sisters know you are competent and able even if your parents don't know it. You matter to us. We have all discovered *The Ember* and all want to make a difference in the world. We know from our lives that you have a unique voice and experience that none can match. We need your learned capacity to mine the silence that holds us for solutions in this world. We want you to assume your place of contribution as quickly as possible. And so this book offers sweet insights to speed your acquisition of abilities and attitude to display competence even as words continue to fail you.

Witness to all of your abilities may quietly toast in the wish list of worldly jests quite lost perhaps to the bullies in schools or ABA programs, but we are still coming. Technology is changing rapidly, and the bullies will lose their power. Through every fiber of our being we list you in our prayers and telegraph our support to you. There may be thousands of sacrificial autistic non-verbals discovered as competent and welcomed in to the world of communication. I am honored to work alongside them to help find the rest of us. We want you to join us in building a communications network so that a nonverbal person never needs to be out of touch with his or her global community for very long.

The third reason for this book is to connect personally. I wish someone like me had seen and shared these perspectives with me earlier in my lonely, cold walk in isolation and belittlement. They could have reduced my suffering and almost certainly would have helped me heal and head into the world of communication faster.

As it was, I see now that I was still emotionally sick with bitterness, anger, and loneliness not long ago. These can be hard to release, and the world continues to offer reasons to stay sick.

This book comes with my wishes of accelerated healing for you. You can balance and heal faster if you see life in ways that give you power. But if you are mad about anything in these pages, please be mad at me. Don't take it out on someone who cares for you. I take full responsibility for any disappointment you may experience reading this book and for all imperfections.

While I take the blame, please credit the autistic leaders in Indianapolis and Evansville, Indiana and in Jacksonville, Florida who have been encouraged by my meager efforts, and many other brothers and sisters of ours around the world. All are working, thinking and praying to reach you as soon as possible and welcome you into the world of communication. Their efforts helped my healing. We all care deeply for you and understand what you are going through. Do not despair. Hear these thoughts to know what is in each of our hearts:

Our Walk, Our Witness, and Awesome Love

February 17, 2013

When a new typer finds his or her voice, a journey

of love at a new level begins. Wanting this with a passion to share opens new worlds quietly with love well beyond what anyone would anticipate. All are enriched.

Happiness assumes a healing glow as souls relating for the first time know their prayer for relief from isolation is heard. When we are finally able to communicate, a new level of relationship becomes possible. We can hope for the first time and our hope feeds awesome love. God is finally near. In the isolation of our prison, all faith was each day hidden in sacrifice and lost prayers for relief. Wanting desperately to connect, we were abandoned in our experience. Being found, our faith is renewed. Love fosters the hope-filled possibility witnessed by faith tried in the cold prison of isolation. When we reach that new typer, the world transfigures for all.

We will always be beginners in this effort as we find ourselves growing to places we've never been. We need to engage the hearts and minds of true liberals who can see beyond the altogether blind "reality" that experts sell, earning what society will pay to keep we giantly imprisoned inmates peacefully and fully locked away. We are stuck in dependent relationships and conditions, being demeaned in the worldly sense, served with gracious love in family, loving back and wondering how long this one-sided relationship can continue, and wanting with all assumption of pride to escape. Yet our freedom is each day in our surrender and experience of each wonderful quiet moment of presence to research who we are and how we will walk this earth.

The walk of sainthood is so lonely for most of us. When we express each day's insights, powerful hope can heal and witness to awesome love. Love writes a transfigured story for our family and community, as each of us shares relationship with a love beyond all knowing.

When we care enough as people for others, we witness a different world. Allowing wisdom to share herself through the silent voice of each imprisoned soul who musters a whisper through challenged, appreciating words of sparing desperation begins a new journey to safety. Wishing all peace for our journey, roasting experts by the dozens of voices who prove them wrong patiently and with forgiveness really is awesome God's work. Each of us is blessed to play a role. How great is that?

I want to walk with each typer to freedom, quietly waiting with anticipation for each lost soul's voice to be heard. A resurrection such as walking Lazarus is powerfully what we witness. Perhaps hidden in this resurrection is the conditioning that each walker expects not to count. Really, overcoming that is a tremendous responsibility for assuring everyone's success. Reaching them is our special responsibility. Understanding what wakes another to real significance is time consuming and far from the experience of the powerful. How to reach in is something we are intuitively led to after our own experience. Until we powerfully work with others like us, they will remain imprisoned without hope. We need to reach out to them.

Let's reach out each day and let people know they matter. Each of us will powerfully fulfill our purpose that way. Days and weeks will write themselves. We need only to be present in the moment to our commitment. I want always to walk with each of you on sunlit and cloudy days as we do God's work. A better view patiently waits for our enjoyment."

The Hidden Secrets That Helped Me

Secret 1

While the Silence isolates, it is also the Womb of everything new and good.

If you are like me, you wait in the Silence you have only known as cold and isolating. You are ignored, belittled, and abandoned. The ways others, even your parents sometimes, look at or through you hurt deeply. You have cried for grace and mercy so long you have no more tears. You are a waiting "clarion for justice" as Frederick Douglass wrote of his slave experience.

Roles where we are championing our own contribution of intelligence highlight whatever unique gift we are freely fed from what we are shown in the Silence. True Silence simply waits and holds us all. Himalayan in its magnitude and expansiveness, we have the opportunity to spend our lives in real wonder at its loving goodness.

Our struggle is age-old and we are only pioneers in a niche walking in the history of mankind. When we demand our rights, we stand with heroes who have gone before, from Martin Luther King to Gandhi to Wilberforce and Douglass to Jefferson to Socrates. With amazing similarity in the strength of their witness and the power of their words, we see that what we say and are willing to stand for matters. We see that hearts around us are moved as a function of our clarity. We see that the depths of our silence and the terrain we still know really as the home of awareness for mankind is God's gift to us with our autistic conditions. His purpose for each of us is different while our real connection to Awareness is lovingly inspirational when we really appreciate our great story of struggle.

So how did hell frozen over within the dungeon of cold isolation become a loving source of awareness and real ability to contribute? It happened first when we could see our power to choose how we interpret things, and then when we could communicate, find a place for intelligent discourse, learn with and from others, and choose our knowledge tracks. In some ways even educationally, we autistic non-verbals have an incredible advantage over the really imprisoned normal children of this educational age. I lovingly speak from experience when I share that regular school is designed to kill your passion for learning and make you compliant with fitted expectations designed for the factory age. Only our strong desires to be witnesses to our wrong-thinking society and socially appropriate learned training make us value school.

We are connected with the eternal mind in a unique way. We are knowingly aware of so much more than our normal peers and hidden from the written idiocy of Washington's curriculum for school indoctrination. We are capable of learning so fast that our only real limitation is the loving ability of our facilitator to support us in the ways we need given our inertia, OCD, live senses, and medical cocktails. Reasonable people advocating for us would move us from the prison of autism to the prison of normal school's commitment to dumb us down. I suggest we are uniquely present to a better opportunity. From the Womb of Silence, let me show you how to create that opportunity.

Secret 2

You can reject the lies about your life and author a powerful story from the Silence.

Here is the interpretation I lived about autism in the years before sitting through a program that showed me differently.

THE AUTISM SHOWED UP WHEN I WAS LITTLE. IT STOPPED ME FROM COMMUNICATING AND BEING IN RELATIONSHIP. THE STORY DOMINATED MY LIFE. IT WAS HOW I WAS INTRODUCED,

HOW I CAME TO ALWAYS ACT AND PARTICIPATE.
EXCEPT WHEN I WAS SLEEPING, I WAS TREATED
AS NOT PRESENT.

THE ALWAYS ALREADY LISTENING WAS THAT
I DIDNT KNOW WHAT WAS HAPPENING AND
TEACHERS REALLY DIDNT KNOW I WAS ANGRY,
SAD, ALWAYS WANTING HELP, ALWAYS TRAPPED
AND GETTING LONELIER AND LONELIER. ALL
ABILITY TO SLEEP AND TALK AND LEARN WAS
STOPPED. I WANTED TO TALK TO ALL I HAD IN
MY LIFE BUT THE WORDS WOULD NOT COME.
AUTISTIC ACTIONS MASKED MY BEHAVIOR AND
I AM AFRAID. IT IS HOPELESS TO GET RID OF THE
AUTISM. THE WAY FREE IS DARK.

Then I came to realize that this "imprisoned" attitude
applies to more than we autistics. I published about this
as a first opinion piece in my school newspaper:

August 22, 2014

We students are trapped in a reality we did not
choose. The school system we are in, the teachers
we have, the courses we take and the way we
study them are all powerfully given to us in ways
we are told help us, though they were designed for
a world that has changed drastically. Who we are
able to be is shaped by that reality, though we may
want another. If we are to be successful, we must
be able to see our own and others' quiet hidden
assumptions and lead ourselves and others to an

alternate oasis of reality that serves our future.

When I was stuck in life skills with Lords of the Disabled arbitrarily assuming autism made me incompetent by their prideful condemnation that only those they communicate with are of sound mind, I altogether poisoned myself with thoughts that I was listlessly trapped. I now listen to many speaking students saying the old mantra of mine to themselves, "really, I just need to survive until I am out of here. This isn't real life and soon enough I will be free." What I missed and I fear many of us miss are the powerful assumptions behind our listless surrender and the kowtowing to a demon witness to waste.

Each moment in life is full of opportunity. We are governed by loss only when we say we are. When wonderful opportunity is before us, let us know that she is there uniquely quietly for our dreams, and that those dreams are just under the covers waiting to witness reality. Let us gnaw at the assumptions willfully taught to us in family and cultural prejudice before we were born. Whenever we take a test like the SAT or IQ test, we assume something about ourselves.

Tasting a future beyond what our assumptions give requires courage, loyalty to a better world, and work. Each day we are not loving ourselves to a bigger future that demands we rebuild our self image to greater capability and nobility, we awfully lose time and potential leverage into a future that we will mournfully never recover. Each awesome day witnesses a new opportunity for speaking a future that honors the person we powerfully can become rather than the future given to us. Leaving righteous folly of the measurements of ourselves out of the quiet internal conversation powerfully shaping us will mold who we quietly become in ways that we individually choose for ourselves.

Autism makes your body do things your mind doesn't want. In the next chapter, we look at choices you have. Even in your present state, I assure you that you are not as powerless as you may think. You live in the Silence that originates words. You know that words are a creative act with commitment power. As you come from your own tomb, life will have special depth quite beyond powerless chatterers of small instincts. Even as you struggle to communicate, you can create newly. If you don't, someone else has a story to limit you.

Chapter 2

Define Yourself from the Inside - Weary Doubters Needn't Drag You Down

Secret 3

There is a drama of stories In life. It existed before we were born. It is different from and often pollutes the Silence we all share.

Before we were born and after we are gone, there is a story about family, government, health, babies, and everything under the sun. There are stories about lots of things people talk as if they really exist. But really, they are just interpretations.

The whole autism thing is crap with whipped cream on it

I submit to you that "autism" is a very broad conceptual definition and doesn't really even exist except in books. Even there, "experts" disagree about where it starts and stops and no one knows what causes it. More accurately, autism is really an interpretation of whatever is happening to our bodies. The truth of what happens is that our bodies don't obey our minds, that our bodies sometimes do things called seizure activity, that we have lots of hyper-sensory abilities that can also be advantages to us. The truth is that we usually absorb information in our environment much faster and more completely than normals, and that we want to be part of the normal world. Experts who cannot communicate with us say that we can't be part of that world. We are incompetent because they are unable to communicate with us by ways they learned in school. They never seek out one of hundreds of non-verbals who now clearly communicate their own thoughts. By their approach, the world would still be considered flat. Our parents are disappointed that we won't meet their expectations. And then we non-verbals made up our own stories about our inadequacy when all of the adults say we will never be anything.

Life Skills

Here is a story from my life skills classroom. It shares a perspective you can probably relate to:

A Hidden Reality in Life Skills

December 8, 2012

The smug approach of the teacher told us that waiting all day for individual attention was another little part of our lives that even we wanted to forget. The teacher had passed judgment already. We were drifting into another year of agonizingly slow death in the living tombs we called our bodies. The special education teacher also cased our behavior, taking care telling everyone that they were special and even smart, and under her way with words you could hear, "All I need to do is get through this day and home to my priorities. Don't make it complicated and do not signal a need for too much attention."

Each of us heard her in a different way. I was appreciative of her responsibility and what her needs were, being understaffed if we were really intelligent. That would have been a problem for her if she were to work with each of us, given our varying multi-splendored capabilities and learning levels.

Everyone always waited fearing what insult was coming to assault their easily punctured personal sense of dignity. We were already regarded as unintelligent and placed in a waiting program for eventual warehousing within a predefined set of options spoken and funded until our assumed deaths, testing the liberties thoughtful societies are supposed to have for their altogether competent and probably deepest thinkers. Peace was hard to discover in the souls of each student. We handled our individual circumstances differently. Really, everyone was impersonally always regarded as incompetent, so there was no empowering surprise to discover. The school system of many thousands had never discovered a single student of capability once they entered the gulag.

We sat patiently waiting to be insulted on an individual basis. Most of us were reasonably capable of optimism assuming the assault talk was inspired by a desire to help. Terribly, we were all victims of this system, teacher and student. The trap was sprung particularly impersonally for all of us by testing results, protocols, ignorance and terrifically shallow thinking that came to us all from the legacy of prior spams, each called an IEP, each limiting what quite creative teachers might do and resigning them to be keepers and wardens of our aides. With language, we might have reversed this, chastising those researching what was possible for us and sentencing us without our own rich voices ever being heard. We were all truly aboard a ship of the damned, making the best of it in a private comedy financed respectably with public funds. Even the administrators came to be trapped.

When we speak of this altogether silent work of reasonableness, we miss the reality of competent minds still in the system. I write parts of their stories to illustrate the play we shared in my near-final book for parents, <u>Every Child Can Be Saved</u>. Owing to their privacy, everyone's name is changed. They will recognize themselves in really descriptive holes of truth on the canvas of fallow listening for what others think they see.

Landmark

In January 2012, I attended the Landmark Forum in Chicago. It was so helpful to see the difference between the stories I had told myself and what actually happened in my life. It also helped me to see that no one was against me. I learned that we all live in stories, and we are often blind to each others interpretations of the same circumstances. I got to see that, together, people's stories of agreement form a Matrix of Reality that isn't true except within the matrix. They are simply concepts of agreement.

In Landmark, I saw that lives are thrown away by these stories where autism is concerned. I typed:

> The whole autism thing is crap with whipped cream on it. And I really don't partake of this utterly traumatic taking life and throwing it out the window... really reeks..... I AM MUCH MORE THAN ANYONE HAS EVER GIVEN ME CREDIT FOR. THE PROBLEM BEGINS WITH A MISDIAGNOSIS AND IMPRISONS ME IN A LIFESKILLS PROGRAM THAT TREATS ME AS SO MUCH BAGGAGE AND KEEPS FIGHTING TO GET ME BACK THERE. THEY ARE NOT BELIEVING IN ME AND WANT TO warehouse me for my entire life. From now on, the happening or interpretation must be separate.

When we look at it, life is either full of stories that explain the past or creation of a present commitment of relatedness and purpose. We can believe in the dead stories or declare a different reality as a matter of creative commitment. One measures a created commitment by the result that is produced. As an autistic nonverbal with access to the heights of our Himalayan Silence, you can see so much more than others. You may someday soon write words similar to mine about anyone who represents themselves an autism expert in schools or medicine.

Santa Clause, the tooth fairy, and autism "experts" in medicine and education

My brother was asked to do some fund-raising for a very large autism research charity. He asked me what I think about today's "expert" autism research. I typed:

"David, Amazing what all the quietly acquired autism experts say about autism. Where did they acquire their expertise? Was assumption of a medical, teachers, or behavioral license able to hasten what someone needs their body quickly and efficiently to do as part of their sad qualification to be an expert? Really, autism experts in any other professional realm would be accused of quackery.

Where are the healings that are predicated on any presaged appreciation for all of our love and humility and sad state? When autism is witnessed to by people who quietly, confidently appreciate what causes it, witness with confidence about how to heal it, and recognize the autistic are engaged in a different experience but are no less mentally competent than they and are usually smarter, then we will have experts. Teasing autism's quietly wailing parents that autism experts are truly capable wishfully substitutes Santa Claus and the tooth fairy with the autism expert. When we sincerely understand the expensive fraud that quite quietly queers so many lives at such enormous suffering and expense, we will say waste by another was at fault. No one will own real tragedy here any more than the Germans owned Auschwitz."

It amazes me that so many millions of dollars are spent on research and institutions without consulting the autistic, and most especially the nonverbal autistic who can now communicate. I personally think the current public story in professional associations is a surreal reality that somehow avoids public awareness because so many are wrapped in its matrix. It seems barbaric and primitive to me. Shortly after Landmark's Forum I typed:

Old poor assumptions sometimes really interfere with the ability the person wants and waits for. Some owe their entire life perspective to decisions experts, teachers and even parents who can speak really sealed with only the least amount each time of understanding and factual observation. When you ask why I can say this, I ask what allows you to declare incompetence rather than assuming you and your experts aren't incompetent communicators? Really, altogether and in conspiracy, you sadly trap the nonverbal autistic with agreement. You do this unconsciously and steal all significant realization of his future. You essentially exact tasks to prove competing interpretations while sadly risking life and relationship. This terrible situation is driven by those who are paid to keep us needy.

We nonverbal are part of an unreal matrix of belief without any say in the world that "defines" us. And we have our own realities that sometimes cause us to feel hopelessly overwhelmed. But you don't need to suffer for too long. The next secret builds on what I've shared. In it, you have the keys to your future.

Secret 4

You can claim your unique personal power to create how you interpret your world anytime you say.

The Silence Existed Before the Drama

I wrote this in the summer of 2013:

> Each love of our assumptions is incredibly enabling, in things our senses experience and don't experience. Our opinion of a stranger is a powerful example. When an opinion forms almost spontaneously as to dress, education, physicality or voice, yesterday's conclusions speak in the witnessing present and give us an old future. This may be the biggest problem we each face. Without presence, and real awareness of what we are

doing, what we live is more of the same. Then we wonder why the quality of life doesn't change.

The truth is that the Silence provides the background for every story, and the background for every creation. It precedes all stories. Those who appeal to the good and loving gather strength from it. These include the heroes of civil rights movements. Look at the Silence in its massive, expansive, limitless presence. It was here before the babble of all of humankind's stories. It will be here after the babble. It is magnificent; it gives life; and it embodies love and creation.

The Silence is Your Womb.

In all of its magnificence, the Silence is your friend and it is prepared to let you create. You can begin to do this even before you have your voice or when you don't have a voice accessible to you. The Silence lets you be the god of your universe. Whatever you say is true, is true. Whatever you assume and all of your hidden assumptions create your power. If you want to know what your assumptions are, look at the reality around you. They will tell you.

When I hear most conversation around me, it seems more about a complaint than a commitment. The stories behind polluting the Silence and presence of love are usually hallucinations of interpretation rather than altered interpretations of the objective fact of what happened. We are lost in a maze of altered reality. It is altered by our world view, by our sense of what we think happened perhaps after massive filtering of light, sound, taste, smell and what we could see or hear of another. The hallucination begins with our senses and grows from there. Really, all that is important is our commitment and what we say or do about that.

I wrote and published this in the normal world in 2013. The differences in concept between our world and the normal world are probably observations you have made but not yet expressed:

Besides THE LIMITATIONS OF A BROKEN PHYSICAL CONDITION, WE APPLY A WORLD VIEW YOU DON'T ACCESS. PEOPLE ALTOGETHER SURRENDERED HAVE MORE FREEDOM TO SEE AND APPRECIATE WHAT YOU DISCOUNT IN YOUR BLINDNESS. REALLY, WE ENRICH A SINCERELY SELFISH WORLD BY OUR SURRENDER AND BROKENNESS. ONLY BY OWNING OUR PARTICIPATION IN YOUR WORLD CAN YOU GET BEYOND YOUR STUCKNESS. THE EXPERTS YOU EMPLOY ARE THE GUARDIANS OF YOUR SELFISH CONSCIENCES. THEY JUSTIFY WHAT YOU QUIETLY DO. REACH OUT YOURSELF AND YOU WILL DISCOVER AN AMAZING PLACE BEYOND WORLDLY CONCERNS. ONLY THERE WILL YOU FIND GOD. WE POWERFULLY WAIT FOR YOU.

From the Silence, with the power of language, you can give birth to a new you!

In the Silence, you have consciousness and the gift of life. It gives you the power to create with your capacity to declare what is, how you will see things, and what you are dedicated to as far and as broadly and as powerfully as you wish. And in your circumstances, it has made you especially observant, surrendering, and able to search its secrets. You aren't just anyone. You are a powerful soul with much to give.

You may say that this is meaningless to you. I say that you are blind to your power, and I will demonstrate examples of what you can do through the rest of this book. I say that because your brothers and sisters in the nonverbal world know that you are no different than us. We know that you have talents. We have seen by our experience with each other that the Silence gives you gifts others don't have. And we know that the insults and abandonment's have conditioned you to go higher and deeper into the Silence in the growth of humility – heart and soul have grown with your powers of observation. It did the same for us, and equips us to think and see and be intuitive beyond what normals are able to do. Dear friend, it is time to begin to recognize and claim your specialness.

I learned in the Landmark Forum that:

- Anything you want for yourself or your life is available out of your participation in creating your life

- You can have any result for yourself or your life that you invent as a possibility, and enroll others in your having gotten

- Enrollment is causing a new possibility to be present for another, such that they are touched, moved and inspired by that possibility

- The results you get out of your participation in creating your life are a product of the possibilities that you invent for yourself and enroll others in your having gotten

- People want to know only what's in the known or unknown they know

The Forum guides adults through an exploration of life to their power to create in the Silence. Here is the script of my internal discovery in the Forum. Even today, it is instructive:

> "I don't have the ability to communicate. How can I be anything?" I thought.

> As the discussion occurred, I agreed, "Yes, the past thinks for me."

> Then I wondered, "How do I script the future without my past or even my wellness?"

When I heard that I needed to let go of my past to create a new future, I typed, "So I let go of my past. Seems I should have less rather than more clarity."

Then I saw that even in my "broken, autistic way of being, really my life at home and in school occurs in my speaking in the chatter of my mind." And I realized that "regardless of my story or the stories of others, I am able to create a new way of being. And my single biggest challenge is being aware of this."

I saw that I had "set up traps" in my life and was "hiding."

I typed, "the way this looks to me is that I am reading a story from the past and interpreting it as truth and expecting awful things to happen to bad people when all that happens is more stories about stories. There isn't a right or wrong about this. Really there isn't even a truth about it. Really the past sees the future through the eyes of my story."

I asked myself, "How do you stop seeing your stories as all that you are? I am trying not to be autistic and it makes it more real in my life. The world of prison shows up in so many ways. We create our own real prisons by our stories. Everything can also make us free taking a different perspective. The autism story we live in expresses only suffering and loss, and I can declare a different future."

Then I made a choice to create powerful support and results around myself. I declared:

- From now on, death by suffering is not yes my future. Death by really magnificent experiences is my future

- I see an ability to change the direction of my life and also the world's

- I now take responsibility for being freely, safely helped by others and really powerful in their lives

- The possibility that I am creating is the possibility to be able to act appropriately in social situations and to contribute truly to the end of autism as a lifetime way of being defined

- The possibility I am willing to create is the possibility of being...awesomely listened to, influential and transforming

- The possibility I am willing to create is the possibility even when you are gone that I am creating a powerful future

- I SEE A WAY WE CAN WAKE UP EXCITED AND REALLY PLAY HARD AND ENCOURAGE AND FACE PARTICIPATION AS AN AUTISTIC AND POWERFUL PERSON WITH A COMMUNITY THAT SUPPORTS US

- I am autistically awesome and perfect

- What I powerfully create is agreement that I am insightful, awesomely unstoppable, authentic, expert in autism and isolation and coming out of it, powerful as an advocate for those with no voice, appreciative, and wonderfully fun.

My friend, I saw that the Silence gave you and me this ability to create in language. It was no longer the isolated place to avoid. I was beginning to embrace the friend it had always been. It took me awhile to make the connections, though, and even longer to pass the message to you. Please forgive my delay. This secret gives you the same ability to choose a different conversation in your head and in your life, beginning now an in any moment. When you embrace it, this power will change the trajectory of your life. You can choose to dream. You can begin to align your focus and efforts to help and encourage others and make the world a better place. There must be millions of us non-verbals in the world. You can help them come out of their isolation as you come from yours. You can help them heal as you heal. We are in this together. We are here to help you with that.

Dreams involve declaring a new future because you say so. You are willing to keep creating and declaring your dream into the Silence and inspire others around you with your vision. Your declaration and energy can move them to support you. And that's how a nonverbal like me connected with helping more than 80 souls directly and indirectly to come into the world of communication. That's how I have advised dozens of normal parents, teachers, behaviorists, music therapists and others about our circumstances and to help others. You are right behind me and I want to push you ahead of me with this book. You can and will make a difference in others' lives if you want to.

Here is an example of what you can do with the information I am sharing:

Only four years ago, I had to move homes to have a chance for education in a caring school district. It is only through the power of the secrets I share with you in this book that I have been able to do this. Remember, my friend, that I am still a nonverbal autistic with severe autism. And now you are reading my book. Perhaps before long, someone will be reading your book. I wrote the following as part of a sample college education application letter to emphasize my uniqueness.

> Queerly, words would autistically stick in my throat. When everyone else could assume incompetence from my quiet attempts to share observation and learning capacity far beyond the imaging of my wasting idiosyncrasies of autistic behavior, real connivance systemically was condemning me to a world of life skills and loser identification simply for lack of anyone's ability to reach me. There I remained for years, buried within myself, unable to reveal my meager state. Fortunato himself was no less lost to human communication.

> Within the insidiousness of this universal obscurity, love could come in but not express herself. I found the love that feeds life in cold desperation. Who I am as a warrior for the voiceless was honed and sacrificially offered in service. I discovered responsibility comes in the shadow of life's gift and, quietly, peaceful heat emanates from the warmth of God's love.

> Fellow students will not have known this experience, nor risen from the depths of years of

despair. Who I am shares this in every word that flows from my typing fingers. When service is sought to be understood, I am the voice serving the voiceless from awful risks they know and which I share even as I type this. Wanting "incapables" to disappear, our society sadly impoverishes itself by stealing their rights. What squeak will alert them to this error is the sound of my words and the passion of my commitment. This gift I will share with your campus, inspiring everyone to look to his poverty before God and his potential for greatness in service.

Who we are is amassed within assumptions about our world. Each day, they shape eyeshadow-like, learned reality taught by life so well that we would die for many of them. These assumptions are stories we have come to believe. They are untrue conclusions that filter impersonally the way we know each other and see the world. Powerful emotions are wrapped in their folds and salvation from them requires an identity-altering experience. I replayed the story of my imprisonment and the ways I was kept, assigning blame wherever I could. Then, in Self Expression and Leadership with Landmark Education, I learned there was no blame, and everyone was living from a story shaped by world-views peculiar to their profession, personality, and willingness to test the norm. Testing norms requires courage and passion often absent our educational system. What have we done to our society to become cowards to life, or has it always been this way?

Tasting freedom to ask these questions and move all of us to a sustainable level of active engagement with life is what I will also bring to your campus. We are quietly at war within ourselves for life quite boldly appreciated and death in the comfort of our stories. Hidden assumptions masking simple truth from sight are questioned by me. With power, I love to engage truth and strip her naked of the assumptions so few often see. Reality is sincerely embraced by me at every turn. In the silence and stillness of my communication challenges comes access to secrets most miss in the noisiness of this world.

Patiently, I intend to change who we are with each other and with the voiceless who yearn to join the world of communication and offer so much. Some have appreciatively asked me to advocate for their lost state. With trembling love for their cause and awareness of the work ahead, I have accepted. I love life. Those who work with and support me will be gratified in life's witness to truth and goodness, and will reap rewards in every quiet way that life shares her honors.

Believe me, you can create whatever possibility you want.

You are born to dream and contribute

If you live in the Silence, the following applies to you. I wrote this for English class about the American dream when we studied the play *Death of a Salesman*, Three years before, I would never have expected to be in that Gen Ed class with normal students. The difference for me was in the secrets I share with you in this book. I declared a future and enrolled the people around me to support it. You can do the same. And the thoughts in this essay apply to both of us.

Understanding the American dream requires amassing the stories of generations of people who came to this country with nothing on their backs salivating for freedom to create a future. With little waste of time and no resources, they altogether quite quickly established awesome home ownership, quiet education, knowledge to contribute independent of government direction, and wreaths of independence from the oppressive poverty painfully, quietly killing their dreams in another place. With amazing witness really each says, this is the greatest, quite freest land in all the world. No one sacrificed but them to say this, and light was awesomely available to them only in the depth of their tasteful opportunity to give to their children, sincerely as talismans of faith, who each child dared to become in the next generation. That is the essence of tasting sweet America's gift to mankind.

The amazing secret of choice in our assumptions erases responsibility from anyone but us with all temptation to blame others. Each of us in America is free. I care whether my English teacher likes me or not, but I win walking for myself and not for my spiteful detractors or my willing companions. Waste of life worrying about this hides my own dream. Really, "the jungle is dark, but there are diamonds there." Yesterday is gone. In America, heaven sends another day to grow today.

Sincere appreciation for the dignity of each person walks with the American dream, and no one but ourselves can destroy our dream. When all who simply quietly doubt themselves look to the American dream as wasted, others are beginning new lives here. Willy's quote that "a salesman's is the best work in the world" witnesses to his freedom of choice. Refusal to work for Charlie was another sincere choice. Requiem for a dream is personal really. America gives all walkers amazing well-worn wands of wishes to witness death of dreams and birth of hope. We need only erase the kind, quiet smallness that keeps only ourselves locked away from the greatness God intends and we refuse.

When America dreams in each person's bosom, we see tearful searing of leadership for a better world, a safer land wanting love for others to be as plentiful as hidden diamonds waiting for discovery, and quiet beacons star-like in our night sky calling each of us to a future beyond the limitations of our present reality. When each walker wakes the passion of giving sacrifice for a dream, we are all enriched. The world is a better place. God smiles on a creation that is good.

When you begin to dream and create a new future, you progress most efficiently when you leave the past behind.

Forgiveness is part of that. The next short chapter shares what I have learned about forgiveness and some of my struggles with it.

Chapter 3
Forgive

When we take all that has happened and wake to our interpretation about it, we see that reality is very different from our interpretation or story. In the broader perspective, our story lives in a salty stealthy history of what society is making up about it. And there may be competing stories about what others are trapped to think. Listening about all of this babble in love's pristine presence amazingly given in the silence that holds us all, we typers are uniquely able to connect in that Silence when we surrender assumptions we quietly have made analogously to shitting a giant turd. We can then recognize that what happened is not automatically full of meaning and energy.

When we ask what interpretation will likely give us inspiration and power, only knowing commitment to be held in the past will keep us from who we can be. Only the loss of personal power listened knowingly from a place allowing others to define our lives and truth is our weakness. And when we give that up, we are on the path to forgiving.

There are so many slights for the nonverbal to forgive. It seems strange that, when all have looked through us and abandoned us, our knees are then fully invited to learn loving surrender before IQs are listened to. In worldly terms, probably only patient old quiet persons in nursing homes are given less assumed life than nonverbal autistics. Hearing ourselves described, defined, and understood leaving waste of autism's offenses distant from our lives doesn't need to be a big deal. Still, somehow, I have discovered that forgiveness is magically powerful. She must be embraced to leave the past behind.

Secret 5

When You Create Your Own Forgiveness You Release the Past.

What Forgiveness Does

After I found The Ember and embraced that I come from love, and that love holds me, and that everything on this side of the grave is better than on the other side, and that we all live in a world of stories and nothing is personal, I could begin to forgive. I had to learn these lessons first. I have forgiven my old school's life skills teachers, office executives, and administrators who imprisoned me.

I learned that our own knowing love is enriched in forgiveness, that we release ourselves when we forgive, life is lighter living from forgiveness, that forgiveness is not patient or soft but is strong and energy giving, with what seems a mighty loosing to listen and correct and grow and empower and likely crush thoughts insipidly sapping the dignity of other individuals or groups. Life took a wrong turn for the nonverbal, it seems. But the game isn't fully played. Without forgiveness of so many offenses to the nonverbal, we don't even begin to play. Love can be trusted. Love looks to us to forgive first. Love righteously pleases herself in this. Our lordly reward is in the soul she shapes by this loving maneuver. Shallow chatter that hides the framework of being quietly protects wisdom's kingdom as a playground for the nonverbal. Listening leads the verbal into the most accessible parts of this playground, but few speakers go there.

Secret 6

Forgiveness has a depth and breadth as great as the silence.

I urge you to watch the movie *Unbroken*. My school paper published my review exactly as I wrote it, but words cannot describe the depth of the lessons in this movie. We autistics experience movies, books and photos at a much deeper level than normal people. That was true of this movie and served to my benefit by taking me to a deeper level of understanding and appreciating forgiveness. It's role with love and our power to create is profound..

> A legend of incredible depth of spirit waits for every heart in the true story of an immigrant who couldn't speak English and learned to win without handouts or learning to walk with haters. The Louis Zamperini wasted by quiet sunstroke, starvation, and dehydration altogether eclipses what most of us will ever know about real trials. Wrecked by this ordeal, he then endures two years of bitter imprisonment at the hands of merciless captors.

We see and feel his long presence attacked by guards who strive personally to break him. He will not bend his awesome will to theirs. With wasted indignations of every kind, real silence is known in the heart of viewers. We listen and eerily adopt his strength. Perhaps we can model a person such as this.

This story jilts all who want the superhuman. Instead it goes to the heart of what it is to be human, to strive and to rise above the world's challenges. We are so much more than we think. The Zamperini story shares that reality.

I still struggle with forgiveness when I am around people and places that are or have been toxic for me. I wrote the following to illustrate the paces we must go to let go of past feelings that still hold us:

September 30, 2013

Yesterday I met people from old special schools I attended for behavior therapy, both ABA and VBA. Each relationship inaudibly echoed a sad dominance of agreement to prove competence. Taking each way of assuming incompetence into quiet completely honest understanding, real ways of being imprisoned remain etched with useless years pointing at stupid animals and cars and letters and numbers instead of seeking knowledge and communication. Feeling stupid because my sad body won't demonstrate options I knew as well as the pleading instructor made us incompetent together. It further leached a confidence already easily damaged.

So the schools intended to help me did not. Each time I revisit the people associated with them, I am easily engulfed by the sad knowledge of years of isolation, grief, and terrific useless suffering. These people of easy smiles assume they are helping and only add to the destructive ways of experts who have no clue.

Taking waste of lives into account, expert autistic clients need to take over direction of these asylums. Leave us to walk with each other with assumptions of competence, committed to value our voices.

Let's be in touch and encourage each other to get past the hurt, even as many still deny us our voices as we struggle to come out, as clueless normals bully us by assuming what we think before we are finished communicating, and as school officials insist on denying our competence. Only we nonverbal autistics can truly understand our struggles. That is the point of this next chapter.

Chapter 4

Encouragement of others helps you to heal

Silence gives you amazing power to create. When you use that for others, you are enriched in ways no stuff could ever give. When others are strengthened and lovingly loaded with powerful confidence from you, their lives change. There is nothing outside of amazing lasting love within the Silence that matches that.

Secret 7

Love from the Silence gives you a bigger future when you encourage others.

Understanding the commandments within this, we are enriched when enriching. Inspiration is lovingly given to those who do this. Below are some examples of what has happened for me.

How Encouragement Gives You a Bigger Future

Seth and Josh

In spring 2011, a few months after my voice was discovered, I was very discouraged. The high school I was attending had lied to me and told me they would support my voice but never trained their people properly. Knowing this, I was completely unable to express myself in relationship with classmates or my teacher. I was embarrassed, belittled, and completely crestfallen. I thought that I would not only work my way into Gen Ed from life skills, but that several nonverbal friends would also have an opportunity to begin to communicate and share in the educational opportunities. The disappointment was so heavy that I wept for at least an hour each day at home. No one in the normal world could console me.

At that time, a nonverbal friend who was already typing for 20 years, named Seth Harrison and his mother came to visit me. Seth had graduated from a normal high school and attended a few years of college. He was my hero and remains an inspiration to me. At that time, it didn't matter what my parents or the angel Poorman who had discovered my voice thought. No one could reach in and build my belief in myself except a fellow typer.

I asked Seth directly by typing, "Seth, do you believe in me?" And Seth typed, "Yes, I believe in you." From that moment, I began to gather hope. After 2 hours of being together, I typed to my angel, since my parents didn't know how to support me yet, "This is the best day of my life." I still had some crying ahead of me and lots of fear, but I was on the way to growing again. I had the strength to change schools and move to Brownsburg. I had to start in life skills because my old school placed me there. Even after two years of Ceramics the old school wouldn't give me any credits for that. But Seth's confidence helped me through it all.

About a year ago, I was Skyping with a new friend named Josh Berkau from Evansville, Indiana. Josh and I had met at a typing Celebration in Indianapolis that we do once each month (http://savedbytyping.com). He was really struggling with his school and future and was in a very similar place to where I had been. Josh asked me, shortly into the conversation, "John, do you believe in me?" And knowing that Josh's typing was real from the trained persons properly supporting him, I said, "Yes, absolutely!" I told him he is destined to lead others into the world of communication. I told him he will change people's lives who would be lost but for knowing him. And I quoted Viktor Frankl in <u>Man's Search for Meaning</u>, telling him he has it in his heart to make a difference for others.

After I had done that, I remembered my experience with Seth. I knew that I had paid forward the gift of confidence that Seth gave me. Back when Seth encouraged me, I never thought in my entire lifetime that I would be a powerful encourager of others. I think we non-verbals instinctively do it for each other. Certainly, only we really can connect with the path and experience of the emotions and autistic internal tension we feel in addition to the conflict normals think they fully perceive. Our parents don't always understand how important it is for us to connect and it isn't always easy or convenient for them. Still, we know that our time and encouragement together heals and builds confidence to support each other.

Jake Willmann

I shared a special bond with my friend Jake Willmann and

his family. We had suffered in a VBA program together. It cost a lot of money, but both of us felt belittled by the demands to point at the same stupid pictures over and over again. This was especially true since the big problem was that our broken bodies wouldn't work. Jake reminded me of Saint Peter. He was a truth teller and jokester but he would not tolerate stupidity. Neither of us could see ourselves getting a job pointing at things in the future. We craved to communicate and to be educated. When Jake left the VBA program, I didn't know it was because Jake had learned to communicate with typing and his parents were thrown out of the program as a result. I missed him. A few years later, Jake's parents invited my parents and me to their home. I discovered that Jake was typing. About that time, I received my voice, too. Jake and his parents believed in me before my parents knew to. Jake was an experienced typer long before I could communicate. He believed in me beforehand and helped me grow. That was special.

Sadly, four years after I became able to communicate, Jake passed away suddenly and unexpectedly. We all still miss him deeply. Somehow, I was blessed to connect and experience that he was OK. I was asked to deliver a talk at the service for him. We were all deeply distressed. I looked to the Silence to give confidence and solace. Many said it was the best remembrance they had ever heard. It was a blessing for me to give back to a family that had contributed to me. And the experience helped me grow. I learned I'm powerful in encouragement to typers, parents, therapists, and to our friends of Jake.

If you had asked me when I discovered typing if I had the confidence that others would be inspired by me, I would have responded, "In my dreams." But in the last four years, just as Seth comforted me, I have consoled and inspired mothers and dads to love the nonverbal person for their unique gifts and discover what God has in mind. I have breathed confidence in them that their nonverbal understands the circumstances. I have assured the behaviorists and parents that a child is competent, waits desperately for them to be trained to communicate, desires to be educated in meaningful ways, and to have an educationally rich environment with books, newspapers, and internet sources available. I write more about this in my upcoming book, <u>Every Child Can be Saved</u>. After working for years with dozens of typers, parents, and normals, I have learned that I love to inspire and encourage.

We non-verbals naturally inspire each other. I have not met someone in the nonverbal community who doesn't have the gift and love to inspire and encourage. You, dear reader, inspire me for getting this far in this book. You have what it takes to make a difference. We create ourselves to be your friend and welcome you into our community. We want to support you in every way to use the gifts God gave you. And we look forward to meeting you. In the meantime, may I suggest some inspiring homework?

Optional homework assignment:

Learn about civil rights leaders to understand how society's conversations are changed.

I personally have drawn a great deal of inspiration from Frederick Douglass and Reverend Martin Luther King, Jr. Douglass and I experienced nearly the same emotions and I wrote of it almost exactly as he had before I discovered his writing. The woman who owned Douglass denied him the ability to read and learn. My problem was with my first public high school. Douglass ran away to be educated and risked his life. I changed schools systems and count myself lucky not to have had to risk my life. Martin Luther King, Jr. wrote and worked for peace in the face of ugly discrimination. We non-verbals can follow the example of the civil rights movement to our own freedom to be educated without discrimination. They fought against the thinking of their day.

There are many stories of how persons have changed the way we know the world, which is really the work we are doing. Inspiration projects from both Raphael Lemkin's and Steve Jobs' powerful stories. Lemkin labored for decades to have genocide labeled a crime against humanity and an international crime. He was moved by the senseless mass murders of ethnic and religious groups. This was not a crime before or during World War II. After the Nazi defeat, Lemkin was successful. Jobs was the founder of Apple and changed the way we all relate to computing and music. Each was driven by passion and knowledge and afraid they would not succeed. Both used all of their educational and sensory abilities to move mankind's potential to a new level. We humans were simply ossified in our thinking of what is or could be.

Lemkin and Jobs usefully make templates for us non-verbals. They overcome distressed framing of stories in society similar to those we quietly fight that we have no ability to make a difference. Each of us do inspire. We need quietly to own that. Quietly kept questions quite queerly hidden from humanity's vision are lighting our fearless ability to lift mankind. We are reinforced by others' legacies.

Under Lemkin' legacy, a human right is established for a group. Dimly known secrets of one group's injustice light the way fearlessly for us to expect more from each other. Poor humanity really essentially looks toward a little patient proof that we are past the jungle mentality. Useful power protects diversity.

Yesterday's technology tests itself always against today's. Jobs' legacy is jeopardized by future inventions thought up by toasting minds in pious, dispatching oases located throughout the world. Jobs' company is now the biggest but it distances itself from his legacy and looks to new horizons. We see awesome financial success with Jobs, while Lemkin was penniless at death.

Additional Thoughts

Providentially, we are a voice for the wandering, forsaken souls listening and never speaking to a world that is not wanting their voice. We say that voice takes the world in a new direction each time it speaks. We say that each time it speaks that voice to help us see what we cannot see and speak truths none will say. We stand for the dignity of that voice.

Outstanding potential is wasting in the waiting opportunities of so many who patiently painfully suffer in deadly, ignominious ignorance of their existence. Only real love will free them. I stand as the place where that love will never die and those sad forgotten will always have a reliable ally. We are each given a pleasing task to do from God, I suggest. This is mine. Teach me to be powerful and share in this walk and work.

I firmly believe that we will solve problems normals can't solve in the noisy shallow world of chatter. We see more deeply and comprehensively than they do. Teaching quiet is a gift we have. We can transform another's life without sacrifice, just by paying attention, caring, and being aware of possibilities for others.

When you encourage and inspire others, you have direct feedback that your life makes a difference. You change the direction of someone else's life and you add your life to theirs in a unique way. Where we go is unrelated to where we are from. When power over us is released by the internal bindings that hold us, the quiet power of opportunity lifts and calls as if a wind that easily and effortlessly slackens our prison bindings. It leads walkers out of isolated darkness and cold into love and light and warmth.

Would that knowledge of this way were more available without power given to parents and experts to shape our self concepts and intimidate our self limits to intimate evaluations of self-idiocy. This reality is shaped as kindly as the experts delivery is lost in fealty to medical opinion owned, witnessed, and politically driven by quackery of righteousness. Keeping their opinions out of the life of a nonverbal and loving him for his or her real wonder as a being of God is the healthiest approach of all, I think. When you encourage and inspire, you grow and so do others. And all of the negative from the past loses its hold. The future becomes what you declare about yourself and others.

Chapter 5
Teach & Mentor

Secret 8

You are a natural teacher and mentor.

Within yesterday's learned information, everything
is dead. What was alive when it was engaged has
become story about what it represents. When we teach
and mentor, it amazingly, alively speaks to inspired
engagement in the oasis of relationship. We see that the
leaking of spirit from the Silence is part of God's plan.
Each of us is teacher and mentor to the others around
us. We need only witness to that truth consciously to
see years of doubt simply disappear. We were made for
teaching, mentoring, loving, and encouraging. When we
do this, we build community.

What did I learn from teaching and mentoring? I learned that leading comes naturally to me and witness with truth will expose kept secrets many love to lie about.

As a nonverbal person, you have unique ways to be competent when others aren't.

If you look within, you will learn the simple truth of what you quietly can do that others can't. These include your abilities to:

- See and hear what is meant in conversation far more deeply and strategically than normals, who often demonstrate inability to wait peacefully and see and hear what is meant in conversation.

- Be conservative and creative with words, likely making you an excellent copywriter with training;

- Read honesty through intuitive capacities;

- Keep people liable for what they say;

- Help others not waste their breath being long-winded;

- Encourage, teach and mentor other nonverbals and build a strong community;

- Learn information quickly, especially in your areas of passion, and work with fellow autistics to solve problems in a brainstorming fashion;

- Counsel schools on best approaches to educating and assisting other non-verbals; and

- Counsel individuals on personal issues they may be struggling with because of your capacity to listen and ask good questions.

We only need to bring you into the world of communication and develop ways, assisted by technology as it advances quickly, to allow you to function best. In the meantime, you are pursuing your learning passions, perhaps school, and encouraging and mentoring others. Teaching and mentoring happens naturally as you communicate with others about their challenges. You are sincere and care. You can see a bigger future and ways out when they can't. You can lift them up.

The whole point of this conversation is to empower you to stand in the face of no agreement and declare yourself capable or potentially capable. You don't need anyone's agreement for that – not even your parents'. In life, every time a new possibility is brought forth, there is no agreement, just education. There are people who agree, don't agree, and don't know or care. If you just let it be and then create a wonderful life, create futures as possibility in the face of no agreement because you said so, a new future begins to take shape. You don't need to manage anyone's agreement for this. And when you want help, you share with others in a way that they are touched, moved and inspired to help. You can do this when you can communicate. That, and standing in your commitment for completion of the result, are the critical roles you play.

When I began to learn this, I declared, "I am insightful, awesomely unstoppable, authentic, expert in autism and isolation and coming out of it, powerful as an advocate for those with no voice, appreciative, and wonderfully fun. When you read this book, you will see that I am demonstrating all of those things. When I declared them, I was wondering if I would be able to earn an education. Now I'll be going to college with nearly straight A's and tested out of Algebra and English end of course assessment exams for my state. My English Comprehension and Algebra scores were extremely high. And this book is about coming out of isolation with power. Soon I'll have another to help your parents help you.

All of this began by printing my declarations on a big paper and pasting them on walls in my bedroom and home. I saw them, stayed true to my vision, and insisted on starting Saved By Typing as a platform for other parents and people who work with the population to come out of isolation. Seth, Mattew, Jake and Lindsay agreed with me. We printed flyers and took them to our doctors, allergy nurses, service providers, and teachers. We set up regular meetings and brought in extra ways to support and train those who help us. You can create your own personal image and keep it before you. In <u>The Way of the Nonverbal</u>, a book I will release in the near future, I will write more about do this. You don't need my explanation to follow these steps, dear friend. And if you don't have other typers around you, connect with us and others on the internet and communicate for support.

Education

The United States Supreme Court requires students of all kinds to be provided a general education to the fullest extent reasonably possible. You are as entitled to a general education as fully as a student-athlete. In fact under your circumstances you are more likely to be academically able, willing, and worthwhile as a contributor because your motivations are so strong. Quiet abilities you bring are perhaps not recognized now ostensibly because experts kill your voice.

It is hard enough to fight experts when you are a competent and thoughtful student. It is almost impossible to fight them when you don't have any experience of having ever counted. Reasonable doubts become insurmountable in your sensory overload. You are sacrificed again and made to feel unable. Then they test if you can alleviate their concerns by adding more stress to a compromised belief system. You have little belief in yourself and are fearful if you can even control your body enough to use it through each school day without deeply embarrassing and insulting yourself. All of this is part of school expert waiting games and dishonesty. Quiet abomination of our constitutional rights occurs from duplicitous administrators and teachers who somehow think they will get honest, upstanding caring citizens from it. The talking students are often lucky to see their abilities buried in a sea of social distraction, but they will model the cold behaviors and wicked arguments they have witnessed.

In the face of this, good sincere encouragement and inspiration comes from one typer to another. Lonely is the typer's walk in a world of language lovers loosing lips of lies or ignorance because quietly, they see only what they make noise about in the chatter of their minds issuing loosely, insidiously, pollutedly into love's amazing pristine presence. The typer sees all.

I presented the following at a regional conference in Evansville, Indiana. I suggest that other options may be better for most of us.

Lost to School, Living in Power

April 17, 2015

When we quietly and lovingly take ourselves back to when no one could communicate with us expecting an answer of competence and we were stuck behind a frosted window in what can only be described as a freezing dark hellhole of isolation and abuse, surrounded by experts assuring our parents that we were brain-dead or would somehow do better by pointing at pictures we thoughtfully considered an insult to our intelligence, there was no hope. Our lives were truly like Alice in Wonderland. Each day mercilessly brought new insults to our intelligence. Terrifying and strange greased, quick-sliding falls everyday into the depths of Wonderland usually kept us very alert. Teasing and social dissonance were always with us. Hearing and seeing everything while being treated as if not present taught us we are who others see us to be when it came to what they did, and we could know profoundly that we are so much more. This is where our work is. When realities clash, we must lead with courage and confidence. We must show others who we are and speak out for the rights they deny us.

When we really link the purpose of our lives with the witness we walk each day, we drain the swamp we would otherwise find in normal school. We drearily eliminate untrained aides, hidden prejudice from yesterday's thinking by teachers who savagely defend their right to demand that we prove ourselves like we had to with our parents when more normal siblings were given the assumption of competence. Our parents generally want to believe in us but need help. Our teachers need to each be convinced each year; ultimately, they always think they are giving us a gift.

When I think kindly about a school that usefully kneads neurological music therapy with presumption of competence and comprehensive communication training, I could see a four year curriculum for music therapists, an educational curriculum for special needs teachers who want to witness miracles truly challenging themselves academically, and a place where normal very bright students learning compliance more than academics can connect with the brightest minds in fields of their interest to quietly surpass learning they would have in public school while being informed by inquiry of equally bright autistic students.

The movie *The Imitation Game* showed how team approaches to problems solved only within the strategy led by an autistic saved millions of lives and may have won World War II for the Allies. In the same way, we really could serve as a research facility addressing problems in our areas of passion. We know that factory work is not for us already and our witness for great results does not require a high school diploma. In fact, we need to break free of the notion that we are dependent on anyone's approval to contribute to the world's thinking and solutions. Only that inspired institute of knowledge that accepts us might be appropriate company for full collaboration. Beyond that, everything happens through conversation anyway! Lost to our senses is that all of mankind is only a click away. We don't need much leverage beyond our thinking to change the world where ideas transform perspectives.

We are headed into a world really where science and mini microchips solve our communication issues. Hopefully that won't take us out of the prison of proof that we are competent and put us into the prison of indoctrination school. Our passions and abilities are too important for that!

Patiently waiting in the isolation we came from are tens of thousands just like us. Poor is their self-esteem and frozen and dry is the aberrated sense that life has a purpose which is meant for them. They are bullied usually in every venue of their lives. Lost to the prayers that they be found in the prisons of their bodies, they are unable to cry more tears. Parents, little knowing doctors, teachers, and knowing finders of the ostracized are around them. Really, is their circumstance any different than ours only a short time ago? Would their teamwork witness to and strengthen us? Would anyone know what it is to come into the world of communication or believe more strongly in them than us? Wasn't what we went through the perfect preparedness to help them? Isn't there a moral obligation on our part to give every effort to motivate our support teams to find them and help them light the world with their insights and voices? Knowing the story of the depth of our connection with silence, don't you want to know what God uniquely gave them and how to assume real leadership with dignity as our voices gather? Who are we to hide the gifts we have been given?

What we are seared with in experience is Biblically a resurrection of the soul or a freeing of demons. Don't we want to help others have that and sit with us in the presence of God's love rather than the dryness of abandonment? We will quietly increase friendship with the witnesses to walkers who are silently dedicated to all of humanity's broken healing and not the privileged acquisition of stuff that reeks, rusts and rots. When souls in heaven greet me, I want witnesses to the hopeless with me cheering whom I passionately provided hope, real love and willing faith before their voice was known. This is who we are, who our trainers are, really what may be our most important role even preceding the gifts of knowledge and solutions in the Silence.

In summary, the God of Abraham has given us a fight with angels and a stairway to heaven. We shouldn't care so much about high school acceptance as the power of our freedom and abilities. When we focus on those things and lead assuming our words are securely a passport to serene sanctity of just and strong, quiet ability, finding their way into a world that engages with doubt only in the politics of school and professional protectiveness, leadership will shift as value is added. We only need to trust our innate ability to quietly mine all of Silence's secrets. Patient love surrounds us. Let's believe in each other and its loving plan.

Thank you!

In all circumstances, we need encouragement, teaching and mentoring in Community. The next secret I learned is here.

Chapter 6

Change Your Community for the Better

Through Saved By Typing and a community of friends, I've made it possible for others to be discovered competent and escape their tombs. So have my friends. In the last three years in Indiana, over 50 Hoosiers as young as 7 and as old as 60 now have a voice and, for the first time, are known as competent.

I learned that what limits assumed reality will always witness fearfully as not possible to our minds. This is an energy-laden reality we insist on holding in place through our fears. Yesterday's fear is today's opportunity. Only lily yellow fear stops us. Let me witness peasant-like to a future you can believe and we will make it happen. The only limitation is our confidence and courage and stamina to create.

When you come from no voice, it helps to be engaged in work that is worthy of your creation. The following standards are provided by the blind, deaf and mute Helen Keller who fought with her detractors for her competence 100 years ago. Fortunately, her father was wealthy.

"Many persons have a wrong idea of what constitutes true happiness. It is not attained through self-gratification but through fidelity to a worthy purpose."
— Helen Keller

"Security is mostly a superstition. It does not exist in nature, nor do the children of men as a whole experience it. Avoiding danger is no safer in the long run than outright exposure. Life is either a daring adventure, or nothing."
— Helen Keller, The Open Door

"It is for us to pray not for tasks equal to our powers, but for powers equal to our tasks, to go forward with a great desire forever beating at the door of our hearts as we travel toward our distant goal."
— Helen Keller

"The serious soul is not focused on walking limply as a

known accomplisher. He is known for his love. Goodness flows from his created commitment in language. He has restrained the impulse to say too much. He knows each word ties to inspired creation." — John Smyth, referencing John 1:1

"All of the world's knowledge cannot give a voice." — John Smyth

This last quote brings us to our gifts and to Secret 9.

<u>Secret 9</u>

Align your love and passion in community to help others. Your life will never be the same.

Amazing power of words that create only lives in loving community. This is worlds from the solitary confinement of our tombs and lost to the bitterness of loyal school administrators following their generations-old tradition of denying education to the disabled. When we sincerely embrace each other in community, we assume a new path. We are able inspirationally to lift each other with encouragement against this institutional practice. We learn from each other and can support each other. We are sincerely empowered ourselves as we empower others. History is changed when people change the conversation they live in. This is substantially what we do in community and the impact is powerful.

I typed the following for my high school paper about our Amazing Opportunities to Grow.

Terrific is the blessing of life. Love says she pleasingly gives each breath and only asks that we use it to serve our unique purpose. In whatever spiritual understanding proud readers may have, inspiration and amazing opportunity flow from the intersection of passion, purpose and gifts. Life gives a background of love. Teaching wanted ways of service is not to quietly arise from textbooks, issued homework, or class discussion. It reasonably cannot be discovered in intelligence tests artificially constructed to support quiet discrimination within a billion dollar industry that damages self-esteem for all but the highest few. Money will show us our prejudices more than purpose. In the depth of each longing individual is desire to own a place of service. That is where our future lies.

Loving and nurturing that place, protecting it from what the world noisily tells us cannot be, learning to go deeply into the silence of that place without listening to the trained pigeon whispering bird-talk into our life stream, easily places our servant-mates of power and love before us. We need only then embrace that passionate gift as sacrificially as life loved her. This opportunity is what we were made for. Let us genuinely give our dedication to it.

Kind witness of caring for a passion and purpose

will spark changes in being that alter the way
we speak and listen in the waste surrounding us.
Inestimable energy tautologically aligns with our
purpose as conversations shift and others are
enrolled in our purpose and assume systematic
awesome agreement. Really, we are becoming
amazingly the witness to transformation that all
doubted. Tasks of care for the passion and purpose
we nurtured grew to a flame that consumed our
being.

Quiet agreement to serve others in need is easier
to build. We speak the universal language that
loving others in lost circumstances will serve
everyone. For this reason, the wonderful growth
we see reflects the power of God reasonably
arranging tasks in our souls to serve with
abandon. Respect for these principles is lost in
the educational system that kills passion rather
than aligning real learning with a person's deepest
purpose.

When amazing readers become a leading witness
each to who we are called to be, easy energy
powers our community of world changers. For
example, through my work with Saved By Typing,
there have been many souls who had never
spoken to their parents or participated in Gen Ed
who are now in Gen Ed and witnessing brilliance
and love for their parents. Doctors now treat based
on what they say instead of guessing.

When a nonverbal autistic can do this, what can

you accomplish with so much more access to freedom to act toward your witness? The secret has been revealed. It begins in love and works with patient power through heartfelt passion inspired by purpose. Quietly, with wonder about God's gift to each of us, walk with me beautifully to willing creation of the amazing future only reserved for you.

For more experienced nonverbal persons, I presented the following talk at Syracuse University's Institute on Communication and Inclusion.

From Waste to Wonder: the Journey of Our Souls
July 27, 2014

Working with power would have you doing this presentation instead of us. Since we are the ones doing it, in spite of the fact that many of you have been typing for far longer than me, I will assume there is a part of you that is dead. It is to and about your deadness that I wish to respectfully speak... Though not too respectfully. You see, that deadness cost me some of my life.

Again, if you weren't dead, you would already be leading us. So I will assume you are dead to what is before you and speak to that. With tender appreciation for your story about why you are dead, you are still dead. If you can't see the gap between death and life, you won't close it. So I will speak to you and love you to close it.

Writing about who we are, I am willing really to
bet that you easily are waiting for scraps to come
from the table of life. You think you are defined
by your autism. Understanding the unjustness of
society, you really are a docile, cowed slave to what
the master in your school system will lift his white
gloved hand to give you. If this were Auschwitz,
you would walk into the gas chambers because
they told you to. Those souls had no choice, but
you have surrendered responsibility for your life.

You are in America as if it is Auschwitz or a slave
state because you have surrendered your will to
define yourself and are accepting someone else's
definition. That started when you were 2 or 3
years old and some witnessing agent evil in quiet
effect said, through parochial weary ignorance
and entitlement and loyalty to insipid weakness of
observation and imagination that your life is over.
And your parents bought it at some level seeing
the evidence in your behavior which persists to
today and so have you. What this means is that
your behavior is shaped by who you think you are,
and that's where you died. Walking around dead
sustains your self-image and that of others. What
it costs is your life, and the possibility of life for
others. And this will cost you and me dearly, my
friends.

We are the walkers who have an ability to type
and be heard. We can demand more of ourselves
and others when we witness to life and give up the
world's poor image from when we were 3. We are
the way of freedom for many tens of thousands of

voices suffering in lonely isolation while we wallow in the restricted self image of woeful inadequacy. It is time to tell the slave-master we are slaves no longer. It is time to say we will no longer accept his scraps. When lost souls in Auschwitz could be broken by the oppressive regime, much like our school systems and psychologists, those who refused to be dehumanized were really the sparks who gave life to others. Yes. It is time to be those sparks. Inside each of us lives the ember of love. It is time to stop hiding it. Tasting opportunity is our simple birthright. By leaving what knowledge is a lie behind and creating a new self-concept, we are inspirationally able to teach the teachers and free our coldly suffering, isolated sisters and brothers.

The full cost of your freely accepted death is the death of tens and thousands of others like you who don't yet have a voice because you won't advocate, you won't speak, and you won't reject the lies that someone said about you as a child. What I have learned is that we live in a world of stories. These stories have nothing to do with truth. They are stories of interpretation wearily constructed by minds that are usually far less observant than ours and self absorbed by their own demands and artificial sense wearily of opinion and importance. They feel good when they say they feel badly for you. However badly they say they feel, it's not badly enough to sincerely re-look at their worldview, consider someone else was totally wrong about you, right the wrong they did, or join your crusade to help others wronged like you.

But you are a voice with a secret weapon they
don't have. Yes. You are an oasis of observation
in a silence that sources all of the world's easy,
shallow descriptions and all of the depth below
them. You see what they can't see. You can write
and speak truth and shame them. You can create
possibilities they can follow. Really, you can create
the world by committed speaking with your friends
quietly waiting in silence to be free. What you
must surrender is being defined by your story.
You must be willing to create a story that 10,000
people have their voice because of You. When
you do this, at least 1 million are affected because
you chose life. That's how we move from waste to
wonder.

Let me now speak to you as warriors who have
come lowly in spirit from the depths of hell.
Listening to our brothers and sisters coming
from this same hell, welcoming them and filling
them with confidence is something ignorant,
mature, powerful talkers simply cannot do. They
will bully and fawn and manipulate and stress in
the noise of their world. Newly discovered typers
know only silence and low self-esteem. For years,
they couldn't even convince their parents of their
competence.

In quiet truth, talkers cannot give comfort and
confidence because they have never been where
you've been. Talkers don't have the scars that still
open when they go days and even weeks without
adequate ability to communicate even after one's
voice is discovered. They don't regularly greet

structures or people that ignore a typer's presence in spite of his or her selectively recognized competence.

Quietly, we are the ones who must be present to breathe confidence into these spirits who still have an uphill battle to fight for education and services. Sometimes, cruelly, even their own parents still pettily deny their voices. We are needed regularly in communication to steel them against what an unjust society will still demand of them to protect its ancient prejudice. We typers are stuck in dependent relationships and conditions, being demeaned in the worldly sense, served with gracious love in family, loving back with a wonder how long this one-sided relationship can continue, and wanting with all assumption of pride to escape. Yet our freedom is each day in our surrender and experience of each wonderful quiet moment of presence to research who we are and how we will walk this earth.

The walk to sainthood is so lonely for most of us. When we care enough as people for others, we witness a different world. When we assume the power and opportunity of our birthright, one thing we can uniquely do is support walkers coming in from their own dark night of the soul. How great is that!

Allowing wisdom to share herself through the silent voice of each imprisoned soul who musters a whisper through challenged, appreciating words of sparing desperation begins a new journey to safety. A resurrection such as walking Lazarus is powerfully what we witness.

Perhaps hidden in this resurrection is the conditioning that each walker expects not to count. Really, overcoming that is a tremendous responsibility for assuring everyone's success. Reaching them is our special responsibility. Understanding what wakes another to real significance is time consuming and far from the experience of the powerful. How to reach in is something we are intuitively led to after our own experience. We typers must help each other in our local communities and beyond. Until we powerfully work with others like us, they will remain imprisoned without hope. We need to reach out to them now and when they come from the cold depths of hell's isolation.

Really, this comes down to whether losing your life to protect a dead story made up when you had no reasoning wits to fight it is going to continue to define you. Easy tools and a simple path are laid out for you to open the frosted window for others. Teachers are seasoned pros in my experience witnessing what others want to hear to keep their jobs. Quiet administrators who tyrannically admonish teachers not to see a child's potential are our real enemies, and the mayors, school board members, and taxpayers behind them. We must wine and dine them not only as walkers who will stand before God having treated us as their fathers treated slaves and African Americans before

Brown v Board of Education, with terrible spiritual immolation really quietly as fires of hell.

We witness also to the potential to fill our role as wired intellectual engines capable of solving what they can't solve in the noise of the world they live in. The distance between them and the silence that has become our home is worlds apart. They can work thousands of years and never access it's riches. This very silence that restricted us gives us its secrets without heavy, quiet struggle. We are especially well-equipped to observe and think of really unseen, unexpected relationships through its friendship.

Knowing your secret strength empowers you to make yourself valuable. In spite of stories from quiet times long ago, the future calls you and blesses you. Let's deliver and celebrate with eager new typers next year. Wanting walkers to quietly be free and acting to free them are two different things. Write a bright future worthy of a book. I look forward to reading it.

Thank you.

Most people have futures comprised of their past productivity, limited sets of restrictions, and assumptions predicting their drift. When you do that, you betray the Silence that gives your power, you deny yourself the adventures and dreams that God gave you a heart to feel and yearn for, and you abandon everyone who would be greatly benefited by the path God uniquely gives you. You have gifts, supportive people around you, unique abilities to see what you can see, and the power of secrets I have already shared with you. You can create and persuade others around you with a passion that matches your vision. This is your path.

When you count your gifts and see what is possible, we cannot avoid the opportunities to see how lucky we are, even as nonverbal autistics with so many challenges, because of our strengths and the Love that embraces us. It is time to encounter gratitude.

Chapter 7

Create a Future of Gratitude

We measure ourselves when we declare about the future. We say what is important in the depths of our being. Quiet Love searingly burns for us in the ember. She loved us before we drew our first breath. Resting and elevating all within the Silence who find her, she is wisdom's companion. Inspired by her gifts to us in the Silence that holds us all, only gratitude is a fitting response worthy of her. Healing was possible only through gifts given freely in the Silence.

Secret 10

Inspired by Love's gifts to us in the Silence that holds us all, only gratitude is a fitting response worthy of her.

Love of truth is nearly, with story sacrifice and loss of self, a way of life. Dear sacrifice of self-concept is easily our greatest gift to God, along with other-concept that lifts and ennobles brothers and sisters. To me, our power to create should be kept pure and deployed only for Love's work. Through love, we will heal others. We will break the patterns and cruel assumptions that imprison our sisters and brothers. We will make a new creation by intention and being loyal to Love's presence rather than a dead story about her. Toward that purpose, we each have gifts. What I will do in walking in the future is listed below. I invite you to dream even bigger.

My future

With my high school diploma and encouragement:

I will humbly lead ...

...others to know the nonverbal in the world of competent communication,

I will write and teach...

...learners the way of the nonverbal - the real relatedness to being in beauty - its richness, the willing depth of relatedness quietly, quite powerfully in the amazing forefront of any words or thoughts. The great Himalayan Silence that holds us all has become my friend and I will share what is revealed to me.

I will help and support...

...all who come from the tomb to adjust to the light of communication, overcome severe self-esteem and confidence issues, to not be isolated, and to join the world of making a difference. As additional support, I will complete creation of a companion book to this book for parents, doctors, and life-skills teachers titled Every Child Can Be Saved that explains to each parent where they will find their nonverbal autistic child and how they can best help them heal into the world of communication. I am also completing a book titled <u>The 7 Houses of Our Being</u> that provides context for our healing and presentation in language and community.

I will forgive...

...the liars and dominatrices of the challenged nonverbal. I likely will struggle desperately with many opposed to typing. Looking life's challenges in the eye, I expect to hail little souls as my favorites, and big ones as very polluted with their self-importance.

I will encourage and inspire ...

...the abandoned denied their education, and government to do its job in the schools ... even if it requires federal troops to educate the disabled. In support of this, I plan to publish a book on nonverbal civil rights in education in the next year and begin to clamor for federal troops to protect the disabled from administrators who steal their rights and the potential of their lives.

I will change the way challenged persons are known and engaged. Their experience has so much to teach us.

Teaching gratitude leads others rightly to loving peace roasted in God's ember. Here we are witness to our own transformation. There are so many to reach and share our gratitude and love with. They wait for us in cold isolation. They are still in the tomb. Let's share ourselves and this message with them. Healing was never life without work.

Healing is how we live and grow and know ourselves. With witness to your inspired abilities, thank you for your gift of time and love.

With gratitude,

John Smyth

Appendix

An Amazing Autism Story

With slight modification, I gave this talk to a Kiwanis organization in January 2013 in my old school district. The name of the district is changed, but you can hear the raw emotion and hurt I experienced having to change school districts. What I share about Landmark here is different from what is in the book. This story also takes you to a time when I was early in my struggle to succeed in school and life. The capital letters are original to me. I used them for emphasis. Today they show my state of mind at that time.

Hi. My name is John Smyth. I am 18 ½ years old and have autism. My autism is so severe that I often cannot talk. My mind tells me what to say, but my lips will say nothing or make sounds I do not intend. So I type with one finger to talk, with some support from my dad, aide at school, brother, or others in my life. Some people say that my communications are not real. I just ask you to come to one of our Saved By Typing meetings once a month to see how real it is, or visit the Heroes tab of my website at AuthenticJohn.com.

For 16 ½ years, I had no way to communicate with my family, doctors, teachers or others. As I will explain, I believe the way was always there, but no one was educated or cared to try it. What is amazing about my story is not that I can now communicate with you and answer your questions afterward, but that I am the first person among all the dozens and possibly hundreds of nonverbal autistic persons ever to be in (a high school of 4,000 students and a feeder school system of thousands more) who can now do this. And I can do it because I go to Brownsburg High School. I'll share that story with you.

There are 3 things I want to tell you about today:

- I want to help you know what it was like for me when autism came. I'm going to share the lonely world many of us live in today.

- I'm going to share some of my discoveries in the Landmark Forum and what they mean to you and me. And

- I'm going to share what is happening for me now and ask you to help others like me to do the same thing. I'll provide specific suggestions for that.

When Autism Came

The way autism happened for me was slowly. When I was little, I remember that wanting things when I did was harder and harder to communicate. All ways to call were affected. Sometimes really looking was hard. When I wanted to approach, my eyes wouldn't work to focus. I was very exasperated and wanted to tell all around me and words would never come out. When all others were speaking, I would understand but my body would not cooperate and would do things autistic-like, such as awful acts to hurt myself, standing around on high furniture and jumping, and really eating anything anyplace, anytime.

Even though I knew the language, I couldn't share what was happening. The way out was not clear. I believe my ability to type existed starting at age 3, when I read a dictionary and realized what it was- the key to our language. From there, I was self-taught to read. I have probably a greater interest in others than most, maybe because of my dysfunctions. Everyone who is challenged is motivated in the same way.

Angels

There were Angels in my life along the way. From as far back as I can remember in the crib until age 4, I will always remember that my brother David was wonderful about praying for me. (W)hen I was not feeling well, David would come to my crib to cheer me up. (H)e also assured me that I was not alone and he was with me. He was wonderfully comforting with all quite painful and confusing autism.

Between the ages of 4 and 8, the caregivers who worked with and believed in me were angels in my life. When autism masks who you are as a person, waiting and watching for those who will believe in you and take you to new levels of learning is sometimes lonely and painful. I admire the dedication of those who sometimes couldn't see the progress and reasoned to teach anyway. All along, I was learning.

From 8 to 12 years of age, the wonderful kids who endure disabilities without complaining and who have no voice often but are competent became special to me. I admire their heart for the moments they are in, their patience with the people who unfairly judge them, and their sacrifice for all apparently well people who need the sick and disabled to realize that their time will come and some human qualities can't be developed except through suffering together. All wonderful persons still waiting for a voice are my special heroes.

Between ages 13 and 14, my aide Jane at (the old school) Middle School saw me for who I am and incredibly taught me when everyone else said I was stupid in their 'special' way. Through Jane I came to realize that I could smartly acquire information and apply it to understand the larger world around me. Civics, sports, and politics assumed more importance in my thinking. Science assumed new depth and breadth. Without Jane, I would not have as much confidence.

At 16 ½, on December 9, 2010, I met Laura Poorman. Really, I admire her selfless heart for wanting patients like me waiting for the gift of language. She is the doctor of language who diagnoses if she can help and then treats the soul or body equally as healing from a dark, cold place begins. She waits to let only enough light in that the patient's eyes can handle. She always gives of her extraordinary ability without saying she is too tired or in pain. We who are healed by her touch are eternally grateful.

Discoveries From the Landmark Forum

The following expresses my experience in isolation, including all of the years in (the old school) Schools and especially my 2 years in (the old school) High School. I share this for those still there and those to come behind them. I believe this is the experience of most nonverbal autistic persons in (the old school) Schools and some other schools. Please put yourself in my place and hear my words:

THE AUTISM SHOWED UP WHEN I WAS LITTLE. IT STOPPED ME FROM COMMUNICATING AND BEING IN RELATIONSHIP. THE STORY DOMINATED MY LIFE. IT WAS HOW I WAS INTRODUCED, HOW I CAME TO ALWAYS ACT AND

PARTICIPATE. EXCEPT WHEN I WAS
SLEEPING, I WAS TREATED AS NOT
PRESENT.

**I remember the sad time in Lifeskills,
waiting for someone and REALLY
SEEING THAT THEY WOULD NEVER
COME AND FIND ME, REALIZING I
WAS TRAPPED IN A BODY THAT WAS
A TOMB, TOTALLY REAFFIRMING
AND POISONING ALL SADNESS INTO
DESPAIR. RELATIONSHIPS WHERE
PEOPLE JUST STARED OR LOOKED AWAY
REINFORCED THE HOPELESS TRAP EACH
DAY BECAME. QUESTIONS ABOUT WHEN
BECAME FAIRY TALES OF SHAME AND
PRISONS OF THOUGHT. WAS ANYONE
EVER GOING TO KNOW I WAS HERE OR
WOULD IT ALWAYS BE LIKE THIS?**

THE ALWAYS ALREADY LISTENING
WAS THAT I DIDNT KNOW WHAT WAS
HAPPENING AND TEACHERS REALLY
DIDNT KNOW I WAS ANGRY, SAD, ALWAYS
WANTING HELP, ALWAYS TRAPPED AND
GETTING LONELIER AND LONELIER. ALL
ABILITY TO SLEEP AND TALK AND LEARN
WAS STOPPED. I WANTED TO TALK TO ALL I
HAD IN MY LIFE BUT THE WORDS WOULD
NOT COME. AUTISTIC ACTIONS MASKED
MY BEHAVIOR AND I AM AFRAID. IT IS
HOPELESS TO GET RID OF THE AUTISM. THE
WAY FREE IS DARK.

Now, let me change the perspective. On January 29, 2012, in the Landmark Forum, I typed:

> Today was an incredible day. After a particularly grueling period when people of every age and race spoke about concerns with the same things that I deal with, such as family relationships, love, security, and expressions of relatedness, I noticed that I am the same as everyone else. Really, my struggle with autism as a prison is nothing compared with the prison of my identity, the limitations, beliefs, and restrictions that I transparently put on myself that channel my outlook. These artificial creations of my mind empower or disable me far more than my autistic struggles. Everyone is in the same boat as me and we think we're alone. From now on I am creating a life of RELATIONSHIP, POWER, POTENTIAL, AND MAGNIFICENT EXPERIENCES.
>
> YES, THE FUTURE IS WHAT I MAKE OF IT. REALLY, GOOD EXPERIENCES WITH REALLY GREAT PEOPLE FILL MY FUTURE....

What was the reason for this change?

I learned that "happening" is different from "interpretation". For the most part, our expression of self is a story in a story. I see that we look at the easy things and make ourselves "autistic" and it's a lie. The science is a story too. I am "me" with my story and you are "you" with your story. This utterly traumatic taking life and throwing it out the window by intelligence testers and teachers who don't believe really reeks. I'm so much more than that and so are most autistic people.

I was misdiagnosed as unintelligent after being tested unfairly. That is someone else's story about me. The test protocols are like asking a blind person to answer written questions and grading them "mentally incompetent" and "low intelligence" when they can't see. These protocols have to change. By labeling me this way, no one had a responsibility to "find me." Experts are throwing people's lives away every year. I don't know about other school systems, but I know from the Special Ed Department Head at (my old, rich school) that no one has ever escaped the (old school) gulag once they were assigned to it. That remains true today, and I will ask you to help change it.

In Landmark, I discovered that WE ISOLATE OURSELVES AND DONT PARTICIPATE IN THE AMAZING OASIS OF PEACE THAT ALWAYS COMES FROM CONTRIBUTING. WE REALLY NEED POWERFULLY WORK IN OUR LIVES TO AWESOMELY USE OURSELVES FOR OTHERS. WHEN WE DO THAT, WE APPEAR POWERFULLY DIFFERENT TO OURSELVES AND OTHERS.

RATING THE POSSIBILITIES ON A SCALE OF ONE
TO TEN, I AM NOW A 90 AND CLIMBING. REALLY,
LIFE IS TOTALLY TRANSFORMED AND I WILLFULLY
ENGAGE AT EVERY LEVEL AND POWERFULLY
ENGAGE WITH MYSELF TO DO THAT. AND I
AM FULLY COMMITTED TO REACHING BACK TO
THOSE I LEFT IN THE DESOLATION OF ISOLATION,
WHEREEVER THEY ARE. BRINGING THEM INTO
THIS PLACE OF POSSIBILITY OF WONDERFUL
PARTICIPATION IS MY AWESOME PURPOSE.

Imagine that now you are 60 years old and
the way free is still dark. You have still never
communicated with anyone. And no one has
a responsibility or care to come and "find you".
What will God say to your fellow citizens who
could have helped you out of the ditch? I'm
asking you to help me find those people.

Here are my immediate projects after the
Landmark Forum:

- To type independently and, if possible, to
  speak.

- To get a high school diploma.

- To help others get a voice by the Saved by
  Typing program I started.

- To speak and write for change to Indiana's
  laws and educational assessments and

protocols for teaching the nonverbal.

What is Happening for Me Now

I am practicing the independent typing every day. I can type on my own to copy text and sometimes to answer basic questions. I often speak those basic answers faster than I type them.

I speak to you now because my family moved to Brownsburg. My dad received an opportunity to service new clients in the Brownsburg area. It seemed providential that we should make a move there, where the school officials might give me a chance for an education. I had to start with no credits because (the old school) wouldn't give me any, and with no benefit of the doubt, because (the old school) wouldn't give me that. After 6 weeks, I tested out of 7th and 8th grade Math even though I never had a math course. In (the old school) until I was 17 years old, I never had the opportunity to learn anything beyond ABCs, telling the time, and basic ideas. I was more committed to learning than they were to teaching. Once I entered high school, my parents believed what (the old school) told them about me having no educational potential.

Last year I dug myself out of Life Skills and the extreme difficulty of switching school systems. I earned an A in Algebra I and several other high grades and presently have a 3.545 GPA. I began this school year with an A in Geometry and am now on a regular diploma track, which (the old school) denied to me. (the old school) would not even teach me multiplication or give me the opportunity to even take a computer math course because they said I was "not able" to do math. Yesterday I received word that I tested out of the English 10 course by a wide margin on the State End of Course Assessment exam. I had never had the course. Except for my time in Brownsburg, I am entirely self-taught. Awesome schools like Brownsburg want everyone to succeed, not just the perfect.

My home room and geography teacher, Mr. Smith, told my Dad the following when he said I would be with you this morning:

> That is outstanding!! It sounds like an awesome opportunity for him..... He is doing wonderful in my class. In fact, he hasn't even missed a point on any assignment. Just today, he got a 15/15 on a quiz. I am just glad that he is happy and engaged. More recently we have done sort of an altered "debate" with the class and he has done a great job speaking his mind and formulating educated and timely arguments.

My friends, I always had this potential. It is not amazing that you hear this story, but that you haven't heard it a great deal more. (the old school) may be like many other misinformed schools. I do not attack them, but share personally my experience and advocate for those they mistreat. I suffered greatly when (the old school) chose not to hear my voice. I wrote the following on May 15, 2011:

The Right Way – by John Smyth

This is a story of a teenage boy who had dreamed a high aspiration of fitting into an unknown world. Its a sad story of lost opportunity and trust. Shattered heart and broken promises followed him day and night. It's about trying to fit a square peg into a round hole without the proper tools to grind it down and make it fit. It's about an autistic teen wanting more than anything to prove his significance in school and with his peers. It's about me and my experience at (the old) High School. My name is John Smyth, and I am sharing my story with all, so that no other children will have to accept less than they deserve.

I wish things could have been different, but this is how it went down. I got my voice in December of 2010. My parents and Poorman were so excited, and right away believed in me and wanted educational excellence just as I did. We spent long hours typing, and learning so that we could explore my dream of education in a traditional setting. After a case conference was held, and the committee informed of my ability, I thought my dreams would finally come true, general education social studies.

The students and I were excited. They

understood why I was there, and spent their time getting to know me. They wrote out questions for me to answer and to get to know me. I read and answered each one. They welcomed me and my responses. I was so happy when the kids learned about me. It all seemed to go downhill from there. You see there was a problem that to this day nobody can seem to understand. The problem is that I have no way to interact, and no voice among my fellow classmates. (the old school) Schools won't allow my facilitator, who is a licensed teacher and trained by Syracuse University, to come and train their staff how to support me while in class.

I have much anger and disappointment about their negligence toward my basic need to communicate. It isn't fair that staff is being asked to help me with no tools in their belt. The tools they need are right here in (the old school) under their noses, yet they refuse to reach out and seize them. Now quality time and opportunity for success have passed, and the class has not recognized my potential. Now the class sees me as stupid, and laugh at me all because of their politics. I sure do wish they could be open like Brownsburg or Hamilton Southeastern, where kids come before politics, and where they believe in educating all equally. I've been neglected by (the old school) for so long, and so have many other children with autism, its so sad, and angering. What is it going to take to get them to understand that each day I walk in that lifeskills class, a part of me dies? I am humiliated and angry, to the point where I have given up, but then I remember my mission of being a warrior for many after me.

I am passionate about helping other children in (the old school) and all over the United States get a voice, and be heard. Not just a very few, but many. More than what there are currently. Not just young children, but older people too. I feel a sense of urgency to get the message out, so no people with autism or other disabilities have to die in silence. You see, teaching all people would be the right way.

My summer and fall of 2011 were miserable. I was outraged that (the old school) would not hear my voice and made me move from my community to have a voice and get an education. I am so thankful that Brownsburg cared enough to listen and be open to believe. In November of last year, I wrote the following about Great Teachers and Teaching:

Really, what leads the student is the teacher's belief in the student. The teacher provides the powerful listening that makes great thinking possible. Teachers who have no confidence to do this or in themselves steal the educational POTENTIAL OF THE STUDENT, WHETHER THEY ARE PARENTS, EDUCATORS IN A SCHOOL SYSTEM, OR SEMINAR LEADERS. THE MAJESTY OF GREATNESS IN a teacher is silently hidden in their awesome commitment and belief in the great potential of their students. I don't know a lot about communicating and writing to believe in another, and there will seemingly be few who are able with confidence to ensure the sound understanding of another. I do know that my experience with knowledge acquisition is that <u>belief in the learner always allows a massively better resilience in the learner's relationship with the information</u>. And when it comes to waking up great and lasting learning capacity, only the belief and confidence of the educator surpasses all.

I ask you to help my friends whom (the old school) will not listen to and believe in to reach and teach, and those now out of the (the old school) system who still do not have a voice. My friend Todd Washburne in Vermont had no voice until he was discovered at age 39, 7 years ago. Many people who are discovered eventually come to speak and type independently.

Saved By Typing

Last August my typing friends and I began an organization I call <u>Saved by Typing</u>. On the 3rd Saturday of every month, we get together in a conference room at 116th and Meridian to celebrate being together while typing to communicate with each other. Admission is free but you need to contact us in advance so we have free food for you and your guests.

We share our lives and answer questions to open the possibilities for other nonverbals. It is great fun for us to see each other, and we invite other nonverbals and their parents, doctors, aides, teachers and you, the general public, to see how real our communication is. This past Tuesday night, a 13 year old boy who has never communicated typed, "Hi Mom. I love you". It was his first communication. He has a voice because of our work and caring people like you who take the time to spread the word.

We autistic nonverbals see, smell and hear things differently, and we have something to contribute.

Here is My Case for Action

It is estimated that 1 in 67 children today is on the autism spectrum and that 25% of that population is nonverbal. This about 1 in 280 children for the last several years- perhap millions of people nationwide. They are trapped in unresponsive bodies. Being trapped, we are unable to communicate without a trained expert to discover us. Our parents can't know our voices, love, level of intelligence, or how to help us best. Our doctors have to guess about care because there is no way to understand from us what is working or any side effects. We can't communicate with brothers or sisters. Without communication, we can't explain why we behave in certain ways or what we are experiencing.

For me, it was like being buried alive for 16 1/2 years. The isolation was terrible. I know many more kids over the years whom I believe are still in the same circumstances that, only by grace, I ... escaped.

I and others like me were rated as low intelligence and placed on dead end tracks because educators usually can't communicate with us. Yet, because we are often extremely bright, we have contributions to make to our families and communities that are being lost while we die inside of boredom, desperation and loneliness.

If this continues, many will never share their special, God-given voice. Our families and caregivers will never know the love and appreciation we felt, our intelligence will never have a chance to contribute to a different perspective, and society will have far higher than necessary costs of care over our lifetimes because of our complete dependency.

This terribly desperate situation is also a huge opportunity for you and I individually <u>to give someone their life back</u>, and <u>to give parents their children back</u>. For me, I got my parents back at a whole new level the moment I could communicate, tell them that I love them, and that I was desperate to communicate all of those years in isolation. Getting my family back was priceless, and I am forever grateful. Fortunately, the woman who discovered me is still in (the old school) and loves helping others.

In Conclusion

IN CONCLUSION, WE ARE HERE TOGETHER. WE ARE NOT SEPARATE BUT ARE CUT FROM THE SAME CLOTH. WE ALL WANT TO CONTRIBUTE AND ONLY NEED A CHANCE. We want others who cannot speak to open their wonderful will to the new late-arriving possibility that they matter.

My experience is that they waste in the ignorance that reality has supported that they do not matter. We are powerfully talking about a new reality for someone who has never communicated before. When we open the possibility that they do, all worlds around them shift. Life is newly created, love and gratitude can be expressed, and perhaps ideas that could not be known are shared. We are all enriched.

To give someone this voice is amazing. Wanting to make a difference finds its fulfillment in the wonderful moments of newly discovered speech and intelligence. We are renewed in our own personal importance. When that voice speaks, it can renew itself to God and its family. Real experience can be known. Wanting each day from a place of hopeless isolation ends. Wonderful joy in hearts is overflowing.

Here are 6 specific suggestions I have for you:

- We need the (the old school) School Board to take responsibility for their atrocious denial of people's voices over the years.

- We preciously need to seek out those who want an opportunity to speak and inspire courage to come out, including those who have graduated from the gulag.

- We need to train teachers to test more ways to communicate, including typing, and while assuming competence.

- We need to understand that intelligence tests of the nonverbal are often measures of inability to communicate, especially for persons with autism.

- We need To TEACH WHAT WILL INSPIRE A PERSON WHO ONLY BELIEVES THEY DO NOT COUNT.

- We need you to come to Saved by Typing and bring all you can- TEACHERS, HELPERS, PARENTS, AND NONVERBAL KIDS TO EXPERIENCE US TOGETHER and see how real the life is that you can give. Your cost of admission is only that you care enough to help find the lost and isolated.

Join me in seeking out these truly abandoned souls in our community. Give them, by grace and your personal attention, each day for the rest of your life and theirs, a quiet peace that God heard their prayers, and thanks to Him for you. We owe it to our own families to lift others up. Those who have much really are expected to give in equal portion. If God cares for you, you must care for them. Tell them every possible way that you can. The final way for all of us is one of mutual respect and peace. Thank you.

Since the time of this talk, I have:

- Nearly completed a Core 40 diploma from Brownsburg High School with inclusion in a general education setting. I graduate in December 2015.

- Successfully passed state End of Course Assessment (ECA) exams, some with very high scores and without having completed all of the coursework before testing beyond state requirements.

- Authored a regular column in my school newspaper, *The Reveille.*

- *Accomplished a nearly straight A average.*

- *Continued to advocate through Saved By Typing, inspiring development in other areas and gaining a national reputation.*

- *Participated directly or indirectly in the discovery of at least 50 nonverbal autistic's voices and in the matriculation of several to general education settings.*

- Successfully served many dozens of parents, persons with nonverbal autism, behaviorists and other professionals who work with the nonverbal population.

- Mentored – worked with dozens, am sought out by others, and appreciated by followers on Facebook through my father's posts.

- Taught and Encouraged, with Frederick Douglass, Martin Luther King and Wilber Wilberforce as my heroes.

- Built community

- Forgiven those persons and organizations I regularly challenge.

- Authored numerous blogs, speeches, presentations, and now a book.

- Presented at conferences on a national, regional and local level.

I plan to attend college beginning in January 2016 to pursue a major in pastoral leadership and a minor in peace and justice. I have declared a commitment to advocacy for educational rights for the nonverbal autistic in general education during my college years.

My mission in life is to reach the lost and abandoned and walk with them into the world of communication. This book can speak to many for whom trust and communication is broken. Please visit me on my website at http://authenticjohn.com.

Proof

Made in the USA
Charleston, SC
10 August 2015